THE ULTIMATE GUIDE TO CHART PATTERNS

STEVE BURNS

ATANAS MATOV

© Copyright 2020 Stolly Media, LLC.

All rights reserved. No part of this publication may be reproduced, distributed, or transmitted in any form or by any means without the prior written permission of the publisher, except in the case of brief quotations embodied in critical reviews and certain other noncommercial users permitted by copyright law.

The historical chart patterns in this book were graciously provided by **TrendSpider.com**

DISCLAIMER

This book is meant to be informational and shouldn't be used as trading advice. All traders should gather information from multiple sources, and create their own trading systems. Always consult a registered investment advisor before conducting trades. The authors make no guarantees related to the claims contained herein. Please trade responsibly.

CONTENTS

Foreword	vii
Introduction	xi

CHART PATTERN BASICS

1. What is a chart pattern?	3
2. Trendlines	5
3. Price Channels (up, down, sideways)	8

BULLISH PATTERNS (UPTRENDS)

4. Bull Flag	15
5. Bull Pennant	19
6. Cup with Handle	22
7. Ascending Triangle	26
8. Measured Move Up	29
9. Ascending Scallop	33
10. Three Rising Valleys	36
11. Falling Wedge	39

BEARISH PATTERNS (DOWNTRENDS)

12. Bear Flag	45
13. Bear Pennant	48
14. Inverted Cup with Handle	51
15. Descending Triangle	55
16. Measured Move Down	59
17. Descending Scallop	63
18. Three Falling Peaks	66
19. Rising Wedge	70

NEUTRAL PATTERNS

20. Symmetrical Triangles	75

REVERSAL PATTERNS

21. Head & Shoulders	81
22. Inverted Head and Shoulders	85
23. Double Bottoms	89
24. Double Tops	92
Raindrop Chart Patterns	95
Conclusion	105
Acknowledgments	109
New Trader U	111

FOREWORD

When I was 12 years old, I attempted to disassemble my parent's television just to see if I could put it back together again. As you can imagine, my father was not happy to find me sitting on the floor holding the front panel surrounded by screws. He wasn't impressed when I tried to explain that I was taking it apart so I could put it back together, and rightfully so, there was no way I could have accomplished that.

More than a decade later I was in my mid-20s staring at a computer screen in my office. I had discovered my first candlestick chart and I was trying to wrap my head around it. I didn't understand what I was looking at, but I had the same feeling that I had as a kid trying to reassemble our television. I instantly wanted to solve the puzzle and figure out how the market worked. Not long after, I opened my first brokerage account at Fidelity and started to experiment with stocks. The first-round trip trade I made was in National Semiconductor, now owned by Texas Instruments. Yes, I lost money on it.

When I looked at that first chart, I'll admit that I had no idea what I was looking at. I didn't even understand what a candlestick represented, or grasp the concept that multiple candlesticks could form patterns. I had no idea that those patterns could mean something, and even be predictive of future results. All I knew was that I wanted to figure out how to make money trading stocks and that this was a stock chart. I bet that sounds familiar.

Trading became a casual hobby for me, something I did periodically. I traded at work and asked co-workers to watch stocks for me when I had to leave my desk. As time passed, I became more serious about trading. I spent my nights flipping through charts, experimenting with various software tools, reading books, scrolling through #fintwits and lurking on websites about specific chart patterns and trading strategies. I tried to absorb as much information as I could, and eventually I was able to go from perpetual bag holder to semi-consistent trader. I managed to avoid large losses, and in some cases I even managed to let my winners run (I still sold way too early in most cases).

During this time, I started to keep a list of things that I hated about trading that could be improved. I had built a lot of software by then and it was amazing to me that there was so little innovation in the space. Other industries were launching rockets into space and automating the deployment of cloud infrastructure, but investors and traders were sitting in basements drawing lines on charts by hand. Why?

In 2016, I decided to turn my hobby into a business and started working on a new software trading platform called TrendSpider. My goal with TrendSpider was to increase the efficiency and effectiveness of daily trading activities using technology. When we launched two years later, the reception was mind-blowing. Today, tens of thousands of traders depend on TrendSpider for their charts, scanners, backtests and alerts every day, and the community around the product elevates everyone higher.

I'm not sharing this backstory just to tell you about TrendSpider, but to explain how I met Steve Burns. Steve was one of the first people in the industry to take notice of TrendSpider. He believed in us before anyone else did, and was a fan of what we were trying to do from the start. It is something I'll never forget, because we were a brand-new platform with no recognition. Steve's endorsement of TrendSpider helped people take us seriously in the early days.

So, it goes without saying that when Steve asked if he could use TrendSpider's charts in the book, and if I would be willing to write the forward, I jumped at the opportunity. A resounding double yes!

Before I talk about the book itself, I just want to share something about Steve. He is an amazing resource to traders. Myself and many others have learned much from him. His website, courses, books and blog educate retail investors about everything from basic concepts like charts and indicators, to more sophisticated constructs like strategies and the subject matter of this book, chart patterns.

After I read an early draft of this book, I found myself wondering what might have been if I had a copy when I started exploring the markets. It probably would have saved me a lot of time and frustration. If you are a new trader who is reading this right now, you're already one step ahead of people who are trying to blindly find their way around a chart.

To borrow a concept from Malcolm Gladwell, technical analysis is a 10,000-hour skill. It takes a lot of time and effort to learn how to read a chart, it takes more work to put those readings into practice, and even more to effectively trade your plan.

Which brings me to my last point. There really are no shortcuts in trading. I mean that statement absolutely and literally. None, zero, zilch. However, there are ways to build an edge through education, dedication, practice and hard work. Learning and internalizing the chart patterns that Steve covers in this book is one way to legitimately get a leg up. If you do it right for long enough, you will develop *super X-ray chart vision,* and you will easily be able to spot patterns on charts.

The market is a machine that transfers wealth from the impatient to the patient, from the unskilled to the skilled, and from the frantic to the calm. Be patient, skilled and calm. Good luck and thank you for reading. Now for the main event...

Dan Ushman

TrendSpider.com
November 2020

INTRODUCTION

Over the last several years, I've enjoyed getting to know, and working with Atanas Matov. He has remained one of my most popular guest writers on NewTraderU.com, and his insight on technical indicators, how to identify and trade a trend and his chart pattern knowledge are invaluable to traders worldwide. After the launch of the incredibly successful, Ultimate Price Action Trading Guide, we knew we wanted to team up again. This chart pattern book is our combined effort to bring a clear and concise explanation of chart patterns to help you recognize charts and build pattern recognition.

Buyers and sellers for each trade execution are always equal, it's the price that changes. Every chart tells a visual story of the battle between buyers and sellers at different price levels. Their decisions create patterns that start to show the current path of least resistance. This book is intended to be a road map for seeing the patterns that emerge on charts.

Using chart patterns will give you an edge because they'll help you trade in the direction of least resistance, profit from momentum, see the potential for a reversal in price action and create good risk/reward ratios upon entry.

This edge will show good levels for entries that allow a stop loss to limit a losing trade, but give enough room for a trailing stop or profit target to create a large winning trade. By finding the best price zones on a chart, you'll be able to execute the best asymmetrical risk trades and be more profitable over time.

I would like to thank Jake Wujastyk of TrendSpider.com for his tireless contribution of historical charts for this book. Jake is one of the best chartists I have every seen, and he was kind enough to share patterns he has watched play out over the past few years. You can follow Jake on Twitter @TrendSpider_J.

And finally, none of this would be possible without the creative and technical work of my wife, Holly. She does a tremendous amount of work behind the scenes, editing, formatting, proofreading and designing. She was the best investment I ever made.

Steve Burns
December 2020

CHART PATTERN BASICS

1

WHAT IS A CHART PATTERN?

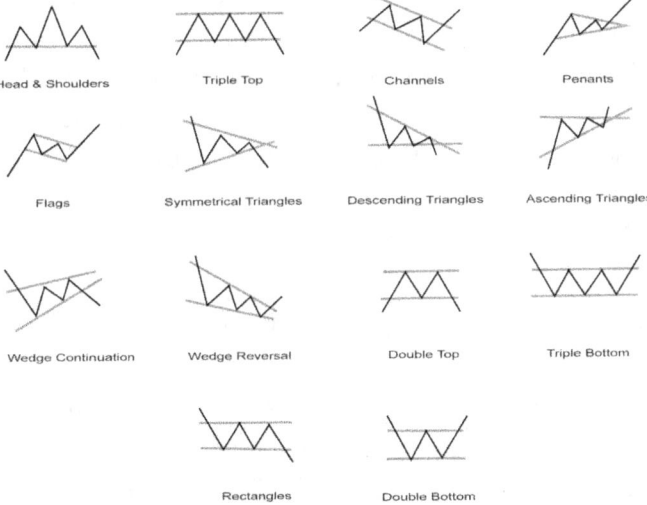

- A chart pattern is a visual representation of recorded price action based on the actions of buyers and sellers in a market.
- A chart is not predictive of the future, but it does show

what's happening with buyers and sellers in the present moment.
- The price action on a chart signals the current trend of a market and the path of least resistance.
- Bullish chart patterns can show when a market is in an uptrend, and it's usually signaled by a breakout of resistance to a higher price.
- Bearish chart patterns can show that a market is currently in a downtrend, and is typically signaled by a breakdown of price below support to a lower price.
- A reversal chart pattern shows that a trend may be near its end and may be reversing.
- Chart patterns are identified by connecting higher highs and higher lows for uptrends, or lower lows and lower highs for downtrends to identify trendlines.
- The primary tool for identifying a chart pattern is a trendline.
- Different chart patterns identify different types of markets: sideways, uptrend, downtrend and reversing.
- The purpose of using chart patterns is to identify current price action patterns and trade using signals that capitalize on them.

Summary

Trading chart patterns is one of the purest and simplest forms of technical analysis and reactive trend trading. Price is your guide and breakouts are your signals. Chart patterns can be used on different time frames in all market environments. Chart patterns work best in markets that trend strongly after a breakout of a range. They breakdown and become less effective in volatile markets when prices reverse into a previous range.

2
TRENDLINES

Types of Trends

- Trendlines are the identifiers and connectors of resistance and support price levels on chart patterns.
- Trendlines are used to measure and quantify the path of least resistance for a chart in your time frame.
- Trendlines are identifiers of the trend in your trading time frame.

- Vertical trendlines must be drawn from left to right to identify if a trend of higher highs is signaling an uptrend, a trend of higher lows for support in an uptrend, a trend of lower lows is signaling a downtrend or a trend of lower highs for resistance in a downtrend.
- Horizontal trendlines must be drawn straight, from left to right, to identify price levels of resistance based on repeating high prices that can't be broken, or levels of price support based on repeating lows that hold.
- Trendlines can connect end of day prices or the full daily range of prices. On candlestick charts, the wicks represent intra-day prices that were outside the open or the close. Both are viable options for trendlines and should be considered inside the context of the chart pattern.
- Trendlines should connect *at least* two price levels in a direct path to be considered viable. The more connections that a trendline has, the more meaningful it is.
- Trendlines must be updated daily to ensure a trend is still in place, and you're looking for a connection and trend of prices in your time frame.
- A break out of price through your connecting trendline can indicate the beginning of a change in trend or market environment. A market could be going from an uptrend or downtrend to a sideways range, as your trendline completely breaks or reverses the current trend.
- The lower green trendlines on this Disney chart represent vertical support of higher lows as the chart shows two uptrends. Notice that price broke back above the red downtrend lines both times before the next uptrend began.

THE ULTIMATE GUIDE TO CHART PATTERNS

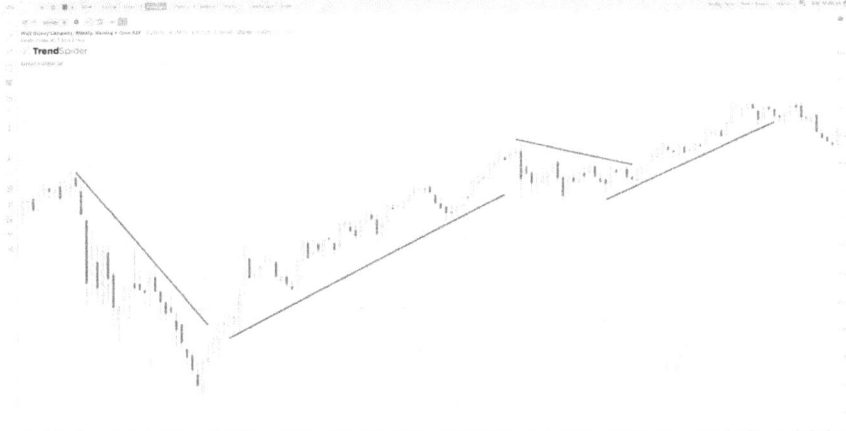

Chart by Jake Wujastyk at TrendSpider.com

Summary

Trendlines are visual ways to measure, identify and track the trends on a chart by connecting vertical or horizontal price support and resistance levels.

3

PRICE CHANNELS (UP, DOWN, SIDEWAYS)

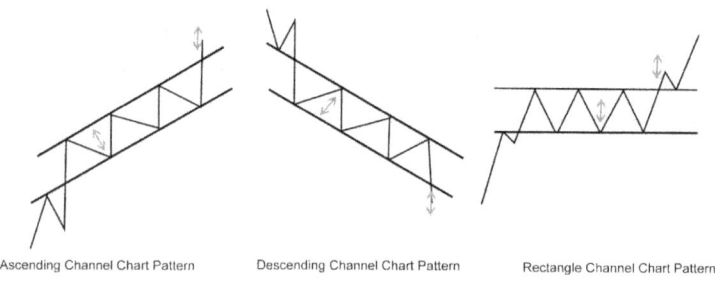

Ascending Channel Chart Pattern   Descending Channel Chart Pattern   Rectangle Channel Chart Pattern

Types of Channel Chart Patterns

When price breaks above resistance, the old resistance frequently becomes the new support:

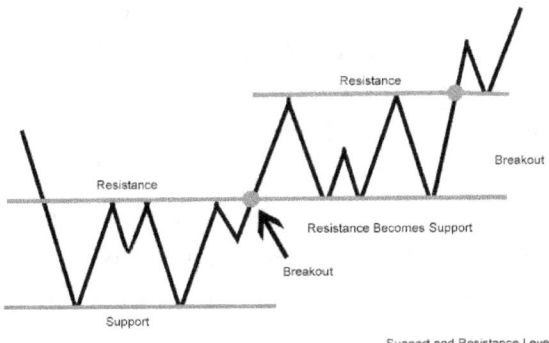

Support and Resistance Levels

- A price channel can be vertical or horizontal and it's defined by upper and lower trendlines.
- Vertical ascending uptrend channels are defined by parallel higher highs and higher lows.
- Vertical downtrend channels are defined by parallel lower highs and lower lows.
- Horizontal descending trendlines are defined by parallel lines that have price resistance around the same area of a high price level, and price support around a similar lower area of price.
- Resistance lines in a chart pattern indicates where buyers are absent at higher prices and selling pressure at those prices set in.
- Support lines in a chart pattern are where buyers overcome selling pressure and step in to buy at a price level to prevent prices from going lower.
- Buyers and sellers are always equal in a trade, the variance is in what price that the trade will take place.
- When a horizontal price channel is broken higher, it often indicates the old resistance is becoming the new support.
- Many times when a horizontal price channel is broken lower, the old support becomes the new resistance.

- Price channels are used to identify where the buyers and sellers were located in the past, thereby defining the current nature of the trend.
- Momentum and trend signals are given when a well-defined price channel is broken.
- Another name for a large long-term horizontal price channel is the rectangle chart pattern. The breakout of the range in either direction can be a momentum signal to enter a trade in the direction of the breakout.

This weekly Apple chart shows examples of two ascending price channels during the long-term uptrend in this chart. This shows the results of tracking the upper and lower trendlines as the lower trendlines held up well in real-time price tracking and connecting on this chart.

The upper trendlines in both channels continued to set higher highs over time, which was bullish. A trader with a long position should look for the lower ascending support line to set higher lows. The lower trendline should continue to have ascending price support at the close of each day.

The upper trendlines in both channels continued to set higher highs over time, which was bullish. A trader who is long a chart also wants to see the lower ascending support line continue to set higher lows by the close each day to keep reconnecting the lower trendline for ascending support. The two uptrend channels were interrupted by a fast swing to the downside, this was signaled by the break of the first channel's lower ascending trendline. The break of vertical support is a warning sign of a possible beginning of a short term downswing or downtrend in price action.

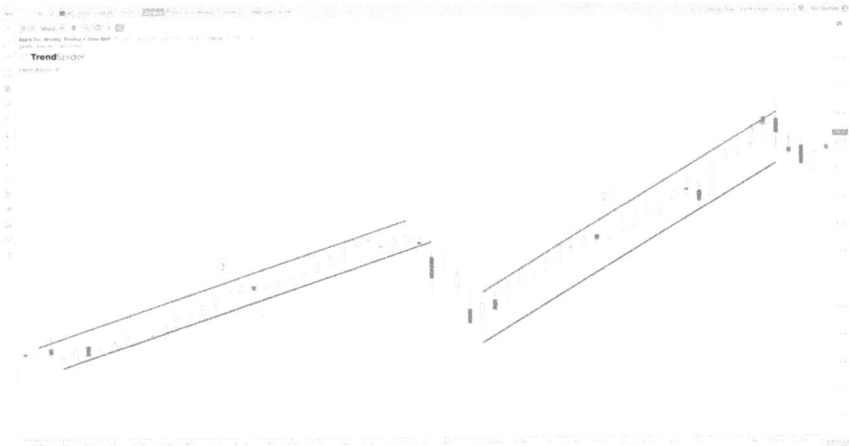

Chart by Jake Wujastyk at TrendSpider.com

This Netflix chart is an example of a reoccurring horizontal price channel that lasted for months. This is an example of a range-bound market. The resistance is near $575 and the support is near $458, creating a wide trading range. Notice that breakouts above this resistance level and below the support level failed over and over again. Returning to the previous price range after a failed breakout is a sign of a range-bound market. Trending markets should have continuation after a breakout is attempted several times. Look for patterns of support and resistance by looking at where the high and low prices were the last few times it made short-term lows and highs in price.

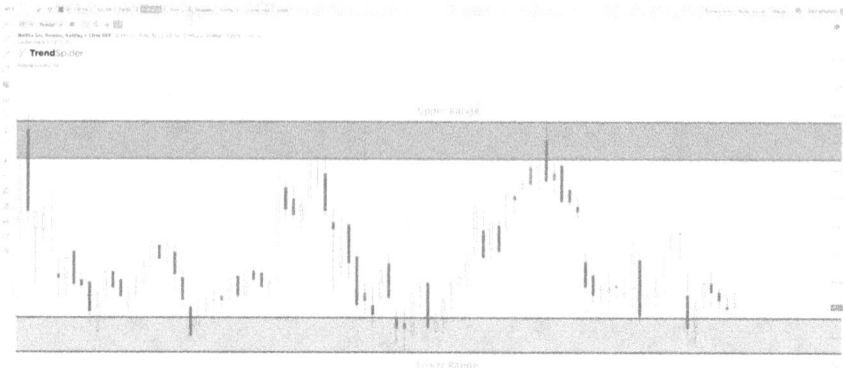

Chart by Jake Wujastyk at TrendSpider.com

Summary

- You increase your odds of success in vertical price channels by buying in the direction of the channel's trend.
- When trendlines connect higher highs and higher lows, you increase your odds of success by buying the dip in price to the lower trendline.
- Increase your odds by selling rallies into upper trendlines when they connect lower highs and lower lows.
- You improve your odds of success in horizontal price channels by buying support and selling resistance.

BULLISH PATTERNS (UPTRENDS)

4

BULL FLAG

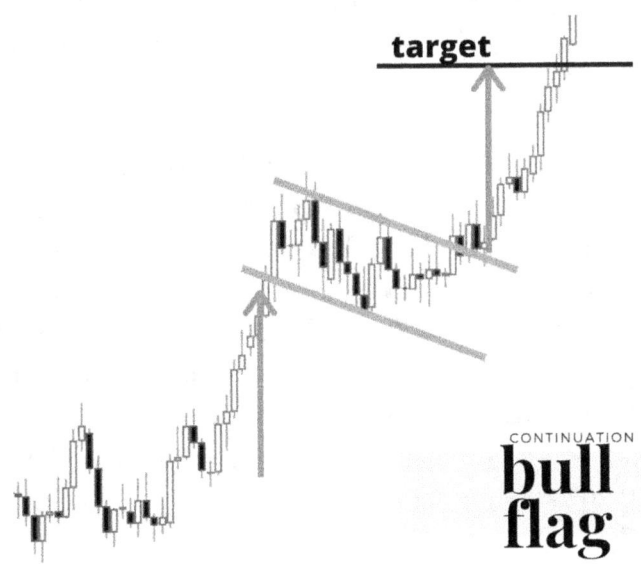

- The bull flag is a continuation pattern of the previous uptrend.
- A bull flag chart pattern occurs when a previous price base breaks into a new uptrend.

- The *pole* is represented by the previous uptrend in price before a price consolidation.
- After the uptrend to new high price stops, the rectangular descending price range is the *flag*. The flag typically has lower highs and lower lows.
- The signal of the end of the flag pattern and the beginning of a new potential uptrend can be seen when the descending upper trendline is broken by an uptrend in price.
- This pattern is thought to be the consolidation of the uptrend.
- The move out of the flag has the same potential magnitude as the uptrend before the flag started.
- A breakout of the flag with higher than normal volume increases the chance of a continuation of the uptrend.
- A stop loss can be set at the lower trendline in the flag after entry.

This Mastercard chart shows a bullish flag pattern where the uptrend begins near $288 and trends up to $314, creating the *pole* of the chart pattern. Then the uptrend stalls and creates the *flag* as a pullback into a descending range. Price broke out at $310 over the upper trendlines in the flag, and then moved in a continuation of the trend to near $368. The pole was a $26 move from the low to the high before the flag. After the breakout, price ran another $58. This is an example of a bull flag moving a greater distance from the flag breakout than it did leading up to the flag.

THE ULTIMATE GUIDE TO CHART PATTERNS 17

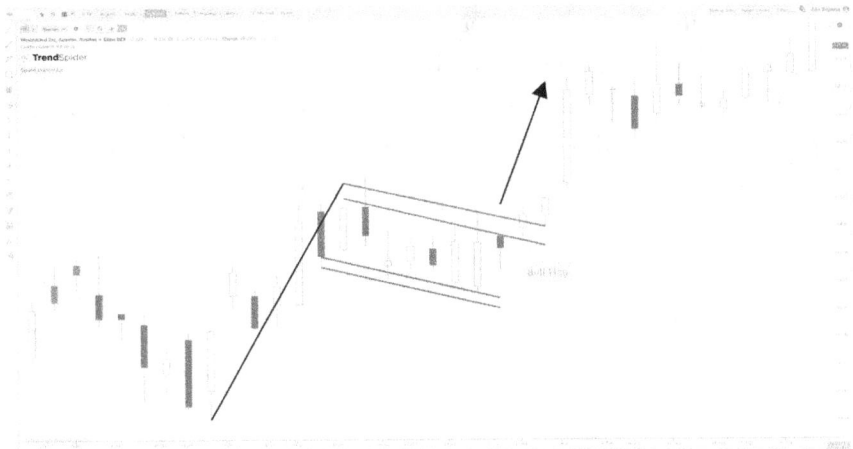

Chart by Jake Wujastyk at TrendSpider.com

Summary

A bull flag is a powerful bullish chart pattern that is found during strong bull markets. These patterns are often formed in leading growth stocks that have gone parabolic.

This is a favorite chart pattern of many traders on different time frames, from day traders to position traders.

5

BULL PENNANT

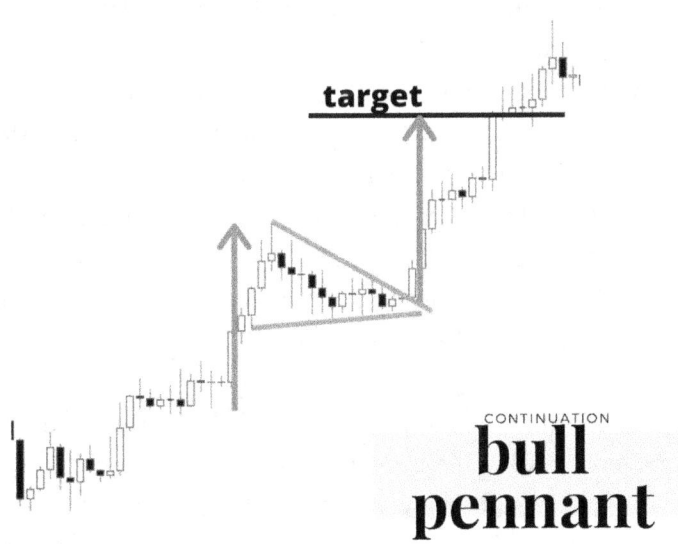

- The bull pennant is a continuation pattern of the previous uptrend.
- A pennant pattern is very similar to a flag pattern, except

- a flag is rectangular and descending and the pennant is triangular.
- A bull pennant chart pattern occurs after an uptrend that follows a previous price base earlier in the chart.
- The *pole* is represented by the previous uptrend in price before the consolidation.
- Overall, the symmetrical triangle of the pennant has lower highs and higher lows that run parallel to each other until they converge at a point.
- A pennant is generally neutral in direction until there is a breakout to the upside that signals it's bullish.
- The signal of the end of the pennant pattern and the beginning of a new potential uptrend occurs when the descending upper trendline is broken with a move upward in price.
- This pattern is thought to be the consolidation of the uptrend.
- The move out of the pennant has the same potential magnitude as the uptrend before the pennant started.
- A breakout of the pennant with higher than normal volume increases the chance of a continuation of the uptrend.
- After entry, a stop loss can be set at the lower ascending trendlines in the pennant.

In this Square example of a bullish pennant the low of the uptrend in the pole is near $151. After the run up in price to the pennant, price stalled over $201. The pennant broke out of the descending trendlines at $180. The price continued to swing higher to almost $200 for a fast $20 gain, which was half the size of the pole before the pennant formed.

THE ULTIMATE GUIDE TO CHART PATTERNS   21

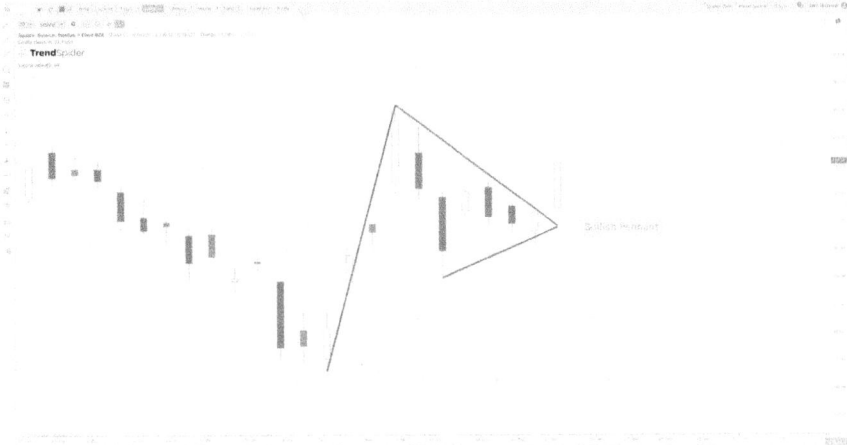

Chart by Jake Wujastyk at TrendSpider.com

Summary

Like a bull flag, a bull pennant is a powerful bullish chart pattern that is found during strong uptrends. They are rarer than a bull flag. The price compression in the pennant can lead to explosive moves after a breakout. These patterns are often formed in leading growth stocks that have gone parabolic.

6

CUP WITH HANDLE

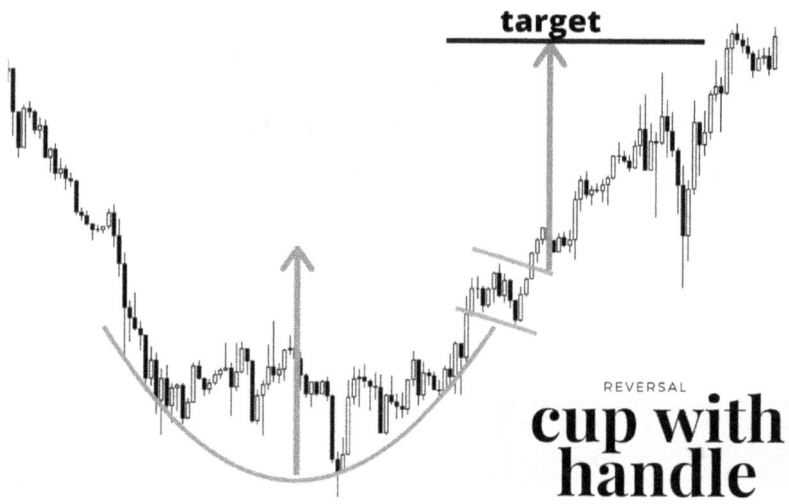

T he cup with handle is a continuation pattern and momentum buy signal as it breaks out of the 'handle' in the formation. It was originally intended to be used with high growth stocks within the CAN SLIM system.

A cup and handle chart pattern ideally takes place at the beginning of bull markets when the stock indexes are trading over their 200-day simple moving averages.

This chart pattern was first popularized by William J. O'Neil in the first edition of his 1988 book, *How to Make Money in Stocks,* and it's one of the newer chart formations. For the best chance of success, the cup and handle setup should ideally come after a clear uptrend. However, the cup with handle is still valid after a downtrend or sideways market. The chart pattern consists of two key components: (1) cup and (2) handle.

The cup part is formed when profit taking sets in or the market is in a correction, with stocks selling off and forming the left side of the cup to the downside. The cup bottom is formed when the stock runs out of sellers at new low prices and buyers start moving in. Buyers bid the stock up again as sellers demand higher prices to sell the stock.

As the stock emerges out of the right side of the cup in an uptrend, it typically fails and meets resistance. It is usually unsuccessful the first time it tries to breakout to new high prices from previous highs inside the cup pattern. This process forms the handle part of the pattern inside a trading range. The second attempt at new highs usually succeeds because there are no more sellers at that price level and the stock breaks out to new highs.

This pattern sets the stage for nice uptrends. The majority of short term traders sold as the stock fell into the cup, the bottom was formed when the holders of the stock refused to sell for less than the support level in the base of the cup, then profit takers were exhausted as the stock came up through the right side of the cup.

The first-time buyers at new highs near the resistance price level above the cup will be the new selling pressure as the second breakout of the pattern is attempted.

The breakout propels the stock upwards and it becomes more expensive because no one wants to give up their long, and likely, profitable positions.

- Cup and handle patterns are not good probability trades if the general market is in a correction or a bear market.
- The pattern has better odds if the stock is in a strong sector that has increasing earnings and good growth expectation.
- The pattern has better odds of success if the stock had a previous uptrend leading into the pattern, showing historical demand and accumulation.
- Check the depth and length of the cup. A cup with handle base usually corrects 20% to 30% from the base's left-side high. Most are three to six months long, but can be as little as seven weeks or as long as a year or more. (William J. O'Neil parameters).
- Look for a classic shape. If you have to persuade yourself that the shape is a cup, it's not a cup.
- Note how much of the cup is in the lower half. A steady climb up the right side is best.
- Look for a 'U' shape and volume that dries up near the cup's low. Volume that dries up at the bottom suggests funds lost interest in selling. U-shaped bases are more likely to work than V-shaped.
- Cup and handle patterns can happen on both daily and weekly charts.
- This pattern has a higher probability of success if the breakout of the handle high happens on higher volume than the 10-day average volume of trading.
- This pattern is trying to capture a stock as it breaks out of its handle and starts an uptrend due to accumulation from money managers.
- The buy point is a momentum signal as the stock makes a new high inside the cup. The stop loss can be set between 7%-10% of the entry price. Proper position size could be 10% - 15% of trading capital.

- A price target could be between 20%-30%, but they can go higher or fall in price and fail.

Activision Blizzard formed a cup on it's weekly chart from November until August of 2019, and then a handle from September to December of 2019 before eventually breaking out.

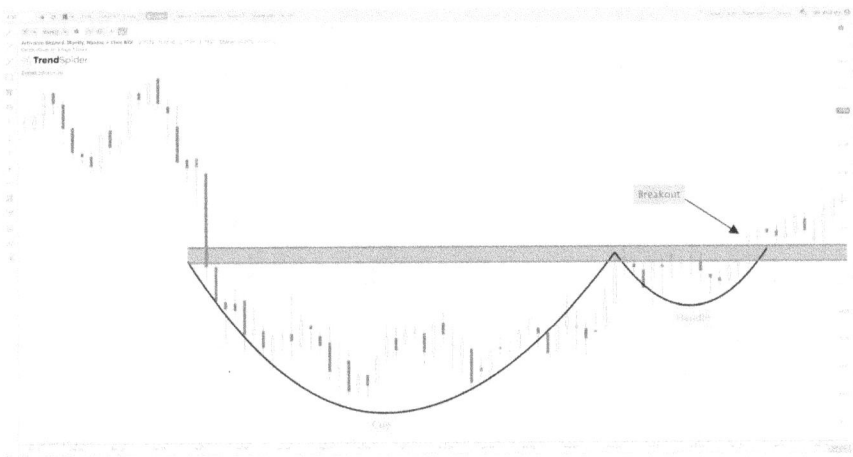

Chart by Jake Wujastyk at TrendSpider.com

Summary

A cup with handle chart pattern is a bullish formation. They have a higher probability of success when following upward trending price action on a chart. However, after market corrections or bear markets, cup and handle patterns will follow downtrends. Some of the most powerful historical cups with handle patterns that led to large moves upward were those that formed over a few months. The older the uptrend in the overall market, the lower the probability the cup with handle pattern will be successful. The volume on the chart should decrease as the price moves down in the cup, and should increase after the breakout higher in the handle when price begins to trend higher.

7

ASCENDING TRIANGLE

- The ascending triangle is a bullish chart pattern that usually forms during an uptrend as a continuation pattern.
- Sometimes an ascending triangle pattern will form as a

reversal pattern when a downtrend comes to an end, but they are usually continuation patterns in an uptrend.
- Regardless of their location during a trend, ascending triangles are bullish patterns that indicate accumulation. The higher lows in the pattern are a clue that sellers are not letting their position go at lower prices.
- The top horizontal resistance line on this pattern holds until the sellers are worked through and buyers come in at higher prices. This signals a buy signal for the potential breakout to higher prices and the continuation or the beginning of an uptrend.
- Ascending triangle patterns can be longer in time frame and wider in range than a flag or a pennant. The length of this pattern can range from a few weeks to months with the average lasting for 1-3 months. The catalyst of earnings will typically trigger a breakout for a stock.
- Volume will often contract as the pattern approaches a breakout. A breakout with higher than average volume can give a buy signal a higher rate of success.
- A return to the breakout price level will often happen as old resistance becomes new support for a second chance entry.
- Traditionally, the price projection for this pattern after the breakout is found by measuring the longest distance in the price range of the pattern, and projecting this as the potential size of a move after the resistance breakout.

This Roku chart shows the horizontal trendlines that lasted about one year in the $177 area, and the ascending trendlines of higher lows that started in the middle of March. The large two-day candlestick bullish breakout over resistance carried through to the middle of September. This chart shows the beginning of a new uptrend in price.

Chart by Jake Wujastyk at TrendSpider.com

Summary

The ascending triangle is a bullish chart pattern with resistance at the top and horizontal trendlines and support at the ascending vertical trendlines that make higher lows. A breakout of resistance is the bullish buy signal. A stop loss could be set if price returns and closes inside the ascending triangle. The gain could be equal to the size of the largest area of the trading range inside the pattern. A price target could be for a run after the breakout equal to the largest point of the trading range of the triangle.

8

MEASURED MOVE UP

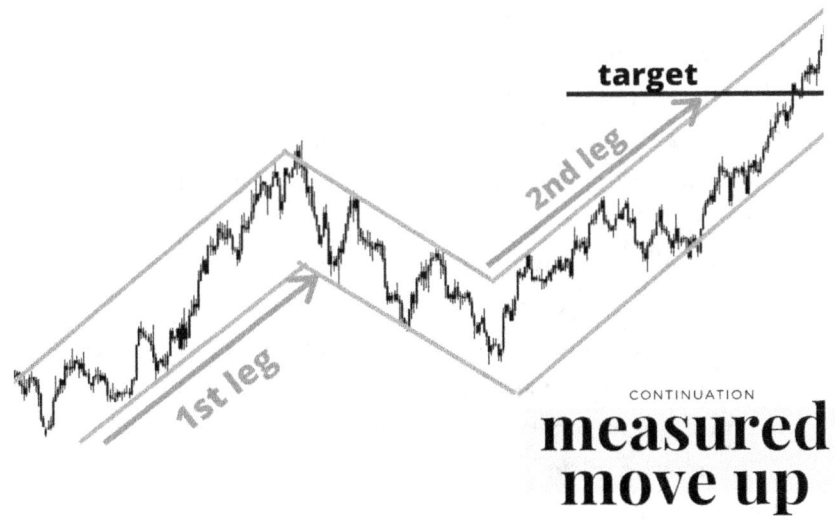

- The measured move chart pattern has three parts, and it can begin as a reversal pattern and then go into a correction before a final continuation pattern of the original uptrend.

- The bullish measured move can't be identified until *after* the correction and consolidation phase.
- The first leg of the advance usually starts around the lows of the previous decline and will likely trend up for a few weeks or months.
- After the initial uptrend, a consolidation or correction is the next phase in this pattern. If it is a consolidation, there could be a continuation pattern such as a rectangle or ascending triangle.
- If this pattern goes into a correction, there could be 33% to 67% retracement of the previous advance, and the possible patterns could include a bull flag or a falling wedge.
- Usually the larger the advance, the larger the pullback and correction in this pattern. A 100% move up may have a 62% correction, and a 50% move up may only have a 33% correction.
- The length from the low to the high of the first uptrend can be used on the low of the consolidation or correction to project a profit target on the continuation of the uptrend.
- If the bullish measured move pattern forms and the consolidation or correction phase evolves into a continuation pattern, then entry points for the next phase of the uptrend can be signaled using the breakout of the consolidation or correction pattern.
- This chart pattern is usually long-term, forming over many months.
- The measured move is a continuation pattern.
- Volume increasing at the beginning of the initial reversal into an uptrend, decreasing as the consolidation or correction comes to an end, and then beginning to increase again with a breakout to confirm the

THE ULTIMATE GUIDE TO CHART PATTERNS   31

continuation of the uptrend, increases the odds of success with this pattern.

This Activision Blizzard chart shows an example of a measured move up on a long-term time frame as a price base. It transformed into an uptrend for months, and then had two months of consolidation and small correction before heading higher after a new price channel uptrend. The clues to look for in the correction/consolidation phase is that the chart quits making new highs for weeks and the bottom ascending support trendline is broken. The pullback phase in this example showed expanded volatility before reversing back into an uptrend with a wider trading range in the second channel up.

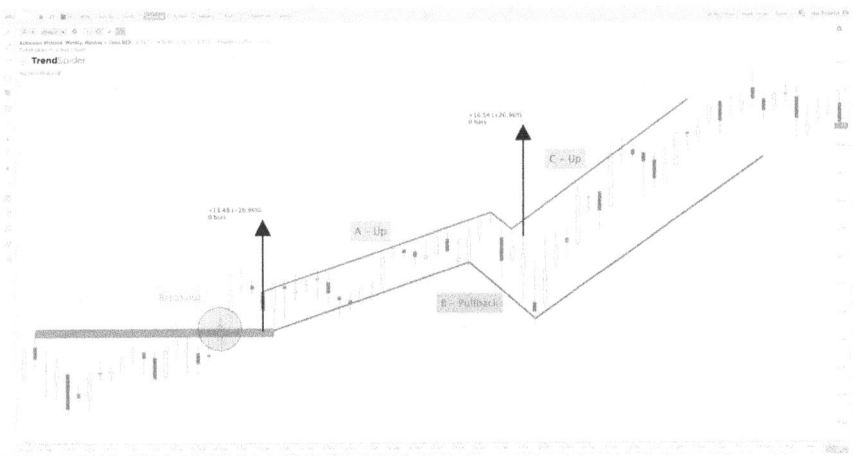

Chart by Jake Wujastyk at TrendSpider.com

Summary

The measured move is a three phase chart pattern that includes an initial strong uptrend coming out of a price base or correction. The next phase starts as the uptrend stalls and either consolidates or corrects. The continuation of the uptrend is confirmed as the consolidation or correction phase is broken out of and the uptrend resumes. The magnitude of the move out of the consolidation/correction phase can be as large as the initial uptrend.

9

ASCENDING SCALLOP

- Ascending scallops are one of the most common chart patterns.
- This is an upward trending chart pattern.
- This chart pattern curves like the letter *J*. The scallop is

formed by two peaks on each side and a rounded lower price support range in between the higher price peaks.
- Ascending scallops sometimes show 'U' shaped volume as the pattern forms.
- They generally don't follow through higher when the market is in a long-term downtrend.
- The scallop price range is wider near the start and finish of the pattern of the curved bottom.
- Breakouts to the downside of the ascending scallop chart pattern can lead to quick drops in price.

In this Zoom chart, you can see the curved price bottom that is shaped similar to a scallop and looks like the letter *J*. It breaks out of the resistance at the high of the scallop upper-end of day resistance in the $225 area. This breakout of resistance started a new uptrend in the chart.

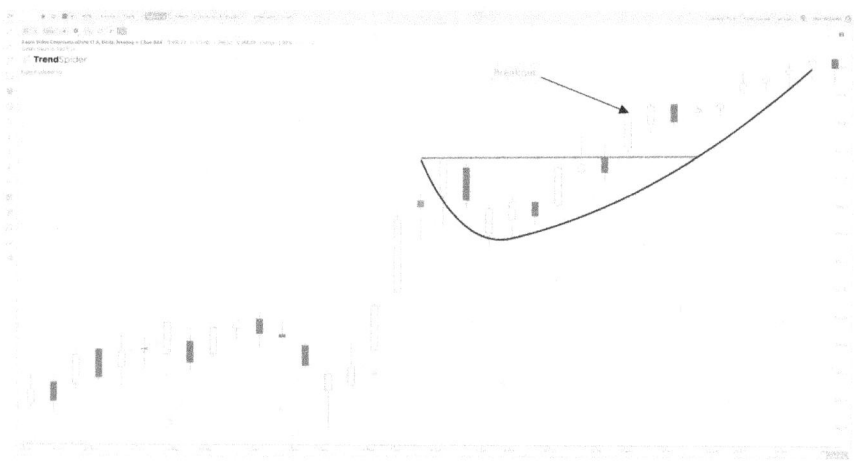

Chart by Jake Wujastyk at TrendSpider.com

Summary

The ascending scallop is a bullish bottoming consolidation chart pattern and similar to the 'cup' in the cup with handle chart pattern. However, in an ideal scallop pattern, this part of the pattern would be wider and more round. It consists of lower highs and lower lows on the left side of the scallop, and then higher highs and higher lows on the right side. This creates a curved scallop shape. The bullish buy signal is a break out of the horizontal line of resistance at the high of the scallop pattern. The old high can be new support if an uptrend begins. A close above the highest price in the pattern signals a breakout to the upside. If this pattern is going to play out profitably, the price should not fall back under the previous scallop resistance line once broken. Downward breakout signals are a close below the scallop pattern's low in price and this invalidates the pattern.

10

THREE RISING VALLEYS

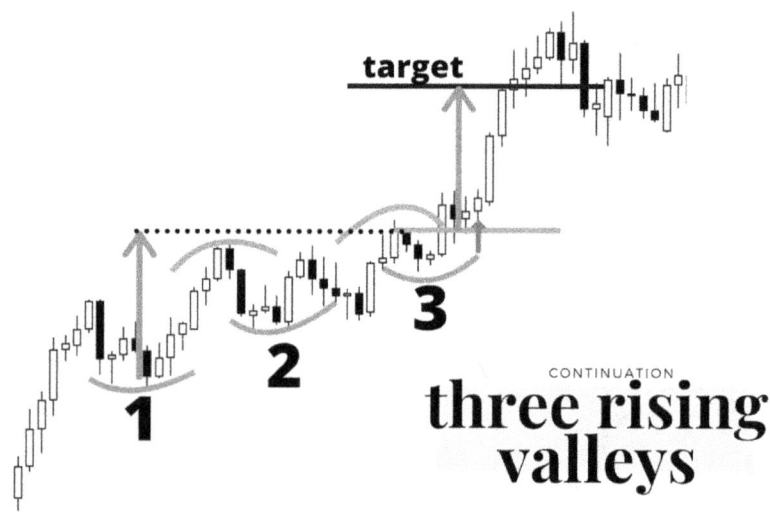

- The three rising valleys chart pattern is one that forms with swings in price during long-term uptrends.
- Most three rising valleys of support qualify for this

pattern. The three dips and peaks in price should be similar in size and magnitude.
- This chart pattern is a good performer in strong bull markets with swings in the trading range before making new highs in price.
- It triggers a buy signal as a valid breakout when price closes above the highest peak in the pattern on the third attempt, after the third low in price.
- Each swing in price from low to high must create a higher low, this pattern can signal a trend change and continuation of an uptrend when three higher lows appear.
- The chart gives a momentum trend signal after the pattern high is broken.
- This pattern can appear on different time frames.
- This is usually a bullish continuation pattern.
- The lows in this pattern are created by three higher low support levels creating three *rising valleys*, with each valley needing to be a higher low than the previous one.
- Each of the three valleys should be very close to the same depth, size and duration. Do not use irregular peaks and valleys when looking for this pattern.
- This chart pattern confirms a momentum buy signal when price closes above the highest peak in the three valley pattern.
- This pattern gives better odds of a winning trade when increased volume follows the trend through the breakout.
- The bigger the uptrend and the more overbought the market is leading up to this pattern's breakout, the more the risk/reward ratio is skewed against you.

This Zoom chart shows the forming of a three valley chart pattern, with ascending support levels around $101, $108 and $133 to create higher lows. The peak near #1 at $165 between the valleys is bypassed by the high of peak #2 at $182 between valleys #2 and #3 to create a higher high. After valley #3, the high of the pattern broke out with a close near $206 over peak #2. After this breakout, a new uptrend emerged.

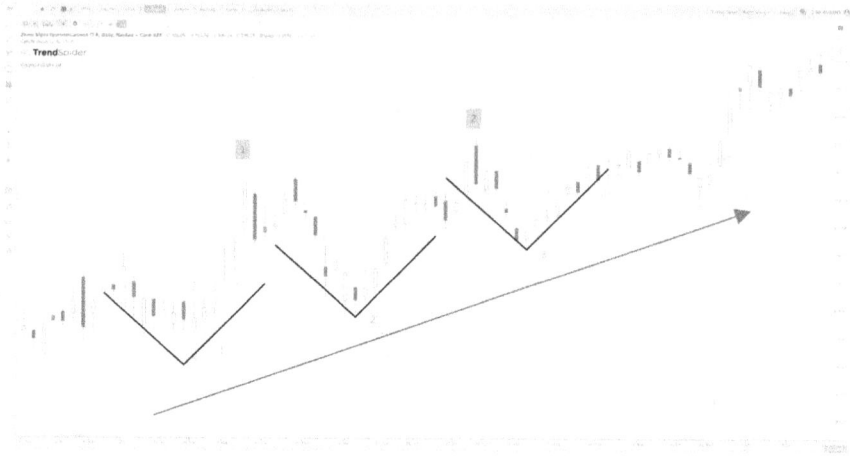

Chart by Jake Wujastyk at TrendSpider.com

Summary

This is a bullish pattern defined by three similar moves in magnitude that each have a higher low than the previous one. These are swings downward in price that don't undercut any previous low. The high peak in price between the second and third low in price should be higher than the high price peak between the first and second low in price. The big picture for this pattern is that there are three higher lows in price and three higher highs, with the third high in price being the momentum buy signal for the next leg of the uptrend.

11

FALLING WEDGE

- The falling wedge chart pattern can fit in the continuation or reversal category. It will trend down when it's a continuation pattern, but the slope in the wedge will be against the overall market uptrend. When

it's a reversal pattern, the falling wedge trends down when the market is in a downtrend.
- The falling wedge is a bullish pattern regardless of what kind of market it occurs in.
- The falling wedge is a bullish chart pattern that begins with a wide trading range at the top and contracts to a smaller trading range as prices trend down.
- This price action forms a descending cone shape that trends lower as the vertical highs and vertical lows move together to converge.
- The bullish bias in this pattern will not be signaled until a breakout back above the descending resistance to show this is a reversal pattern from lows in price.
- This is usually a long-term pattern that forms over a three to six month time frame, but it can also appear on shorter time frames.
- This pattern creates lower lows, but the new lows should have less magnitude. Less depth in lows indicates a decrease in the strength of selling pressure, and should create a lower trendline of support with less declining slope than the upper line of resistance.

Notice that the SPY chart below had lower lows and lower highs for several weeks creating descending upper trendlines. This chart pattern remains in place signaling a downtrend in price until the upper descending trendlines are eventually broken by price to the upside. The break above the resistance line is a signal that the downtrend could be reversing, creating a potential signal that a new uptrend has begun.

THE ULTIMATE GUIDE TO CHART PATTERNS 41

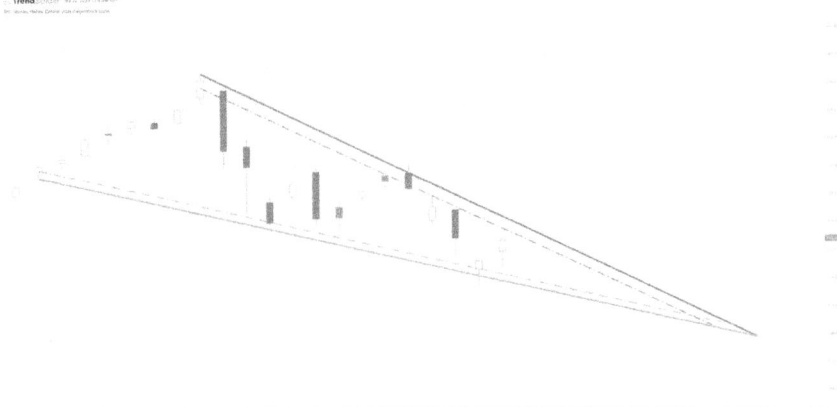

Chart by Jake Wujastyk at TrendSpider.com

Summary

The falling wedge is generally a long-term bullish chart pattern that has a declining line of resistance and a declining line of support. The reversal back above the descending upper trendline resistance is the bullish buy signal, it's not a pattern to buy during the downtrend. The lower support trendline should become more stable and flatter as the pattern forms showing selling pressure decreasing. As the lines converge the odds are that if the descending line of resistance is broken, the pattern is either a continuation of an uptrend if it's a bull market, or a reversal from a near term price bottom if the pattern forms during a bear market.

BEARISH PATTERNS (DOWNTRENDS)

12

BEAR FLAG

- The bear flag is a continuation pattern of the previous downtrend.
- A bear flag chart pattern occurs after a downtrend indicates that a new price base failed to hold support.

- The *pole* is represented by the previous downtrend in price before a consolidation.
- The *flag* is a rectangular ascending price range after the downtrend to lower prices stops. The flag generally has higher highs and higher lows.
- The signal of the end of the flag pattern and the beginning of a new potential downtrend happens when the ascending lower trendline is broken with a new move downwards in price.
- This pattern is thought to be a failed reversal to the upside after a consolidation of price in the downtrend breaks its price support.
- Traditionally, the next move down out of the flag can have the same magnitude as the downtrend had before the flag began.
- A breakdown of the flag with higher than normal volume shows distribution, increasing the chance of a continuation of the downtrend.
- If a short position is entered on the flag support break under the lower trendline, a stop loss can be set with a tight stop on a price rally back into the trading range, or the higher trendline in the flag.

In this Boeing chart example, a two-week bear flag after a previous downswing in price shows that a trend of lower lows started to emerge day after day before the price had a sharp break to the downside out of the bear flag. Some of the clues to the potential of a new leg of the downtrend were the four out of six days of bearish red candles before the large red candle sell-off after the bear flag was broken.

Four days of consecutive lower lows occurred before the formation of the bear flag started. After the breakdown of the bear flag, price fell dramatically and volatility increased. After one more drop in price the chart stopped going lower and the next price range held and rallied. This bear flag and the bearish candles were a warning sign before the large plunge in price.

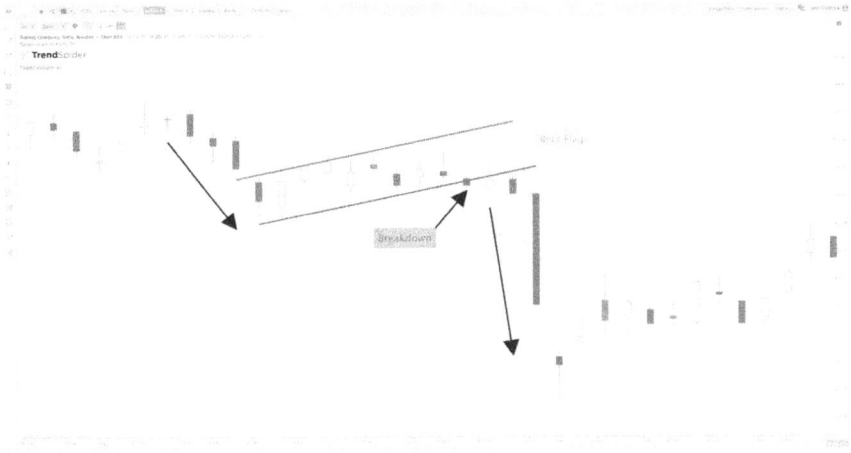

Chart by Jake Wujastyk at TrendSpider.com

Summary

A bear flag is a powerful bearish chart pattern that is found during chart downtrends and bear markets. These patterns are often formed in growth stocks and market sectors in distribution. As market cycles change, this pattern can go parabolic to the downside with oversold technical indicators of little use in finding a bottom in price. The downtrend after the bear flag is often very close to the same magnitude as the downtrend before the bear flag formed.

13

BEAR PENNANT

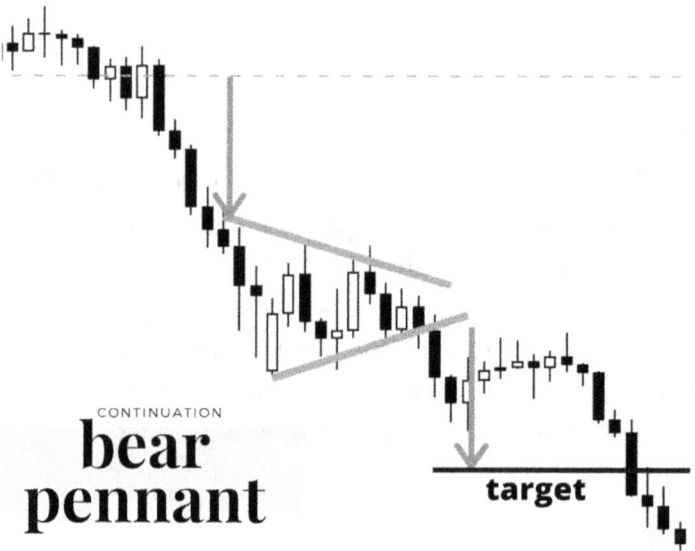

- The bear pennant is a continuation pattern of the previous downtrend.
- A pennant pattern is very similar to a flag pattern except

a flag is rectangular and descending and a pennant is triangular.
- A bear pennant chart pattern occurs after a downtrend out of a previous price base.
- The *pole* is represented by the previous downtrend in price before the consolidation.
- The symmetrical triangle of the pennant generally has a compressing price range of lower highs and higher lows that run parallel and move towards each other.
- The pennant itself can be neutral in direction, but it can be slightly up or downtrending.
- The signal of the end of the pennant pattern and the beginning of a new potential downtrend is when the ascending lower trendline is broken with a move down in price.
- This pattern is thought to be a short-term consolidation inside an ongoing downtrend in price.
- The breakout of the pennant trendline may have the same potential in magnitude as the downtrend before the pennant begins.
- A breakout of the pennant with higher than normal volume increases the chance of a continuation of the downtrend.
- If a short position is opened on the breakdown of the pennant support level, a stop loss can be set at a price return back above the lower ascending support trendline.

This is an example of a bear pennant that formed on the Bitcoin chart during a downtrend in price. After the clear downtrend in the first half of January, a bear pennant formed in the second half of January before the downtrend continued in early February. Price finally rallied in the second and third week of February for a swing back to the upside.

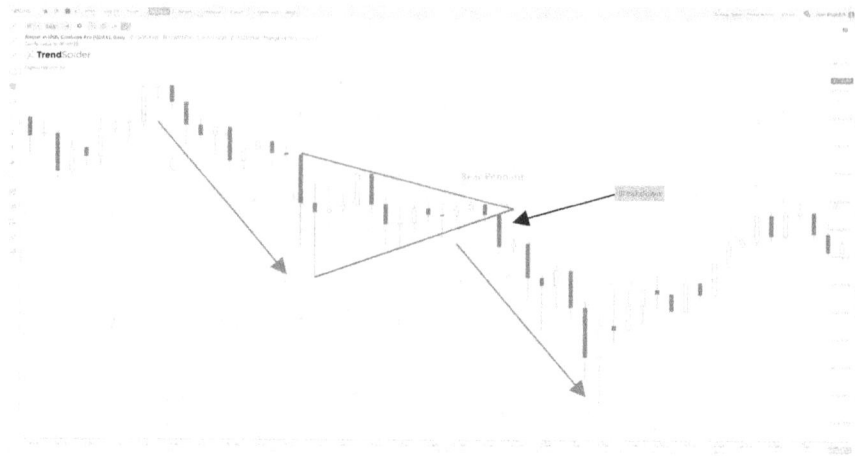

Chart by Jake Wujastyk at TrendSpider.com

Summary

A bear pennant is a powerful bearish chart pattern that is found during the beginning of downtrends and bear markets. They are similar to the bear flag and are the inverse of a bull pennant. They are rarer than a bear flag. The price compression in the pennant can lead to explosive moves once there is a breakout to the downside. These patterns are often formed in leading growth stocks as they begin to go under distribution from sellers unloading large positions. They are also seen on the first leg down in a new bear market.

14

INVERTED CUP WITH HANDLE

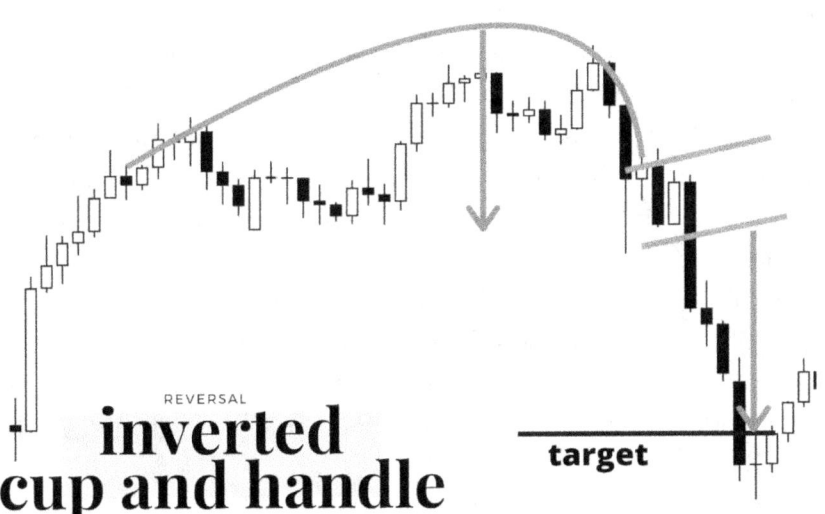

The inverted cup with handle is a reversal pattern and momentum sell short signal as it breaks below the *handle* in the formation. It is typically a topping pattern after a strong move to the upside that signals the end of an uptrend on a chart.

An inverted cup and handle chart pattern ideally takes place at the end of bull markets when the stock indexes are near all-time highs in price.

In order for the inverted cup and handle short setup to have the best odds of success, it should come after a clear uptrend has been in place. The chart pattern consists of two key components, the rolling over price action nature of the inverted cup, and the failed rally in the inverted handle.

The cup part of the formation is created when profit taking sets in on every attempt to make a new high in price, and the market begins to slowly go into a distribution phase instead of rallying to new highs. The cup top is formed when the stock finally runs out of buyers at new high prices and sellers start moving in and bidding the stock down.

As the stock emerges from of the right side of the inverted cup and begins to fall, it fails to move down and meets support the first time it tries to break out to new lows in price. This is when the pattern forms an inverted handle inside a trading range. The second run at new lows is usually successful because the majority of buyers have been worked through and the stock breaks down to new lows.

This pattern sets the stage for a large downtrend because the majority of short term traders bought as the stock fell out of the bottom of the inverted cup. The top was formed when the potential buyers of the stock on the sidelines refused to buy the highs of the resistance level at the top of the inverted cup. New buyers were finally worked through as the market fell below the right side of the inverted cup.

Buyers at new resistance highs near the top were the last buyers of the chart because it failed to breakout of the inverted cup pattern due to a lack of buyers at those prices. The chart then swings down in price as stop losses and trailing stop signals are triggered for exits.

- Inverted Cup and handle patterns are not good

probability trades if the general market fails to go into a pullback or correction.
- The pattern has better odds of playing out as expected if it belongs to a lagging stock in the market with declining sales and earnings.
- The stock should have a previous uptrend leading into this pattern.
- Look for a classic shape. If you have to convince yourself that the shape is an inverted cup, it's not an inverted cup. The trendliness must curve up and then down like an upside down cup.
- Look for an inverted *U* shape and volume that dries up near the cup's high. Volume that dries up at the top suggests funds lost interest in buying. And inverted U-shaped bases are more likely to work than inverted V-shapes.
- Inverted cup and handle patterns can happen on both daily and weekly charts.
- This pattern has a higher probability of success if the breakdown of the handle low or support of the bottom of the cup lip happens on volume higher than the 10-day average volume of trading.
- This pattern tries to capture a stock as it breaks down out of its handle and starts a downtrend due to distribution from money managers.
- The entry is a momentum short signal as the stock makes a new low outside the bottom of the inverted cup. The stop loss can be set on the top trendline of the inverted handle.
- A price target to the downside could be between 20%-50%, but they can go lower or even higher in price into the inverted handle and fail. A trader must let winning trades run and cut losing trades short.

This Exxon Mobile chart shows an inverted cup pattern from January through May as new highs failed to hold and price fell after the peak. From June to mid-July, an inverted handle formed inside the range of the inverted cup, which looks like a vertical ascending price range channel. The breakdown of the lower vertical trendlines support signaled a new downtrend in price action from the middle of July and through August.

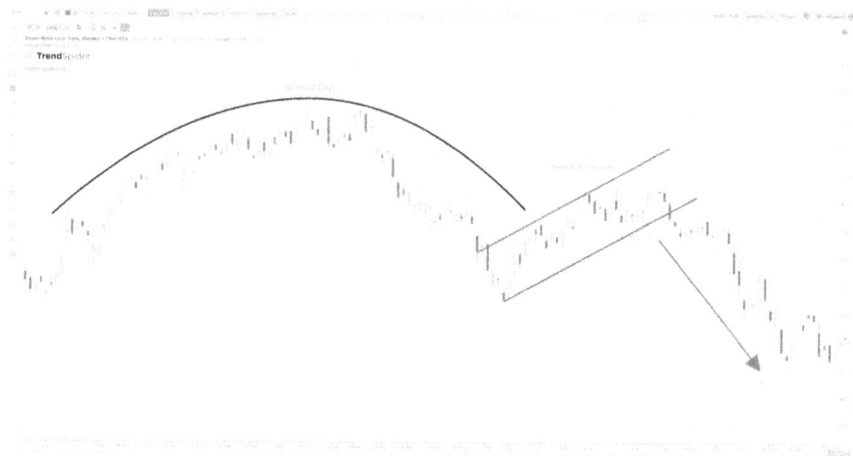

Chart by Jake Wujastyk at TrendSpider.com

Summary

An inverted cup with handle pattern is a bearish reversal topping pattern after a long bull market uptrend. The slow rounding, inverted cup top shows distribution as it fails to make new highs in price. The inverted handle is similar to a bear flag or bear pennant that rallies but fails and falls through the low of the handle pattern. This pattern is used to sell short after confirmation that the inverted rally fails and the low of the inverted cup lip trendline is lost.

15

DESCENDING TRIANGLE

- The descending triangle is a bearish chart pattern that usually forms during a downtrend as a continuation pattern.
- A descending triangle pattern may form as a reversal

pattern when an uptrend comes to an end, but they are typically continuation patterns in a downtrend.
- Regardless of their location during a trend, descending triangles are bearish patterns that indicate distribution. The descending upper trendlines in the pattern are a clue that buyers are not accumulating positions at higher prices as the top of the pattern makes lower highs.
- The bottom horizontal support line on this pattern holds until the buyers have worked through all sellers at that price. The breakdown of the lower line of support signals a sell short signal for the potential of lower prices and a continuation, or the beginning of a new leg in a downtrend.
- Descending triangle patterns can have longer time frames and have a wider range than a bear flag or a bear pennant. The length of this pattern can range from a few weeks to months, with the average lasting 1-3 months. Many times the catalyst of bad earnings will trigger a breakdown for a stock. A news event may cause the breakdown for other types of markets like commodities or currencies.
- Volume will often contract as the pattern gets near a breakout as highs continue to trend lower. A breakdown with higher than average volume can give a higher rate of success for a short sell signal.
- A rally and return back to the breakdown price level is typical, as old support becomes new resistance for a second chance short sell entry.
- The price projection for this pattern after the breakdown is typically found by measuring the longest distance in the price range of the pattern.

This Schlumbuger chart shows a descending triangle pattern in mid-January through mid-February, before breaking the lower vertical support line to the downside in late February. The red descending trendline shows lower highs, while the horizontal green line shows support through the triangle. The breakdown happened before the apex of the triangle was complete. A descending triangle can breakdown at any time, and a trader needs to identify them by connecting multiple lower highs and multiple horizontal support levels in price. The triangle will likely not connect until after the breakdown. An apex breakdown does create a higher probability and clearer pattern, but a plunge to the downside can happen at any time during the formation of the pattern.

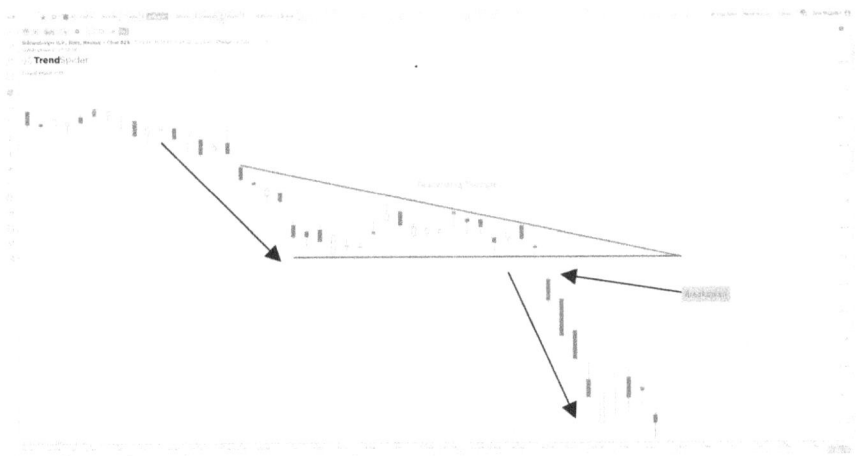

Chart by Jake Wujastyk at TrendSpider.com

Summary

The descending triangle is a bearish chart pattern with support at the bottom on its horizontal trendline, and resistance at the descending vertical upper trendline that make lower highs. The pattern shows that buying power is declining as each rally is lower in magnitude, but the market has support near a key price level. A breakdown of support is the bearish short sell signal. A stop loss could be set at the point that price returns and closes above the ascending triangle support line. The gain could be equal to the size of the largest area of the trading range inside the pattern. A price target could be for a move lower, after the breakout equal to the largest point of the trading range of the triangle.

16

MEASURED MOVE DOWN

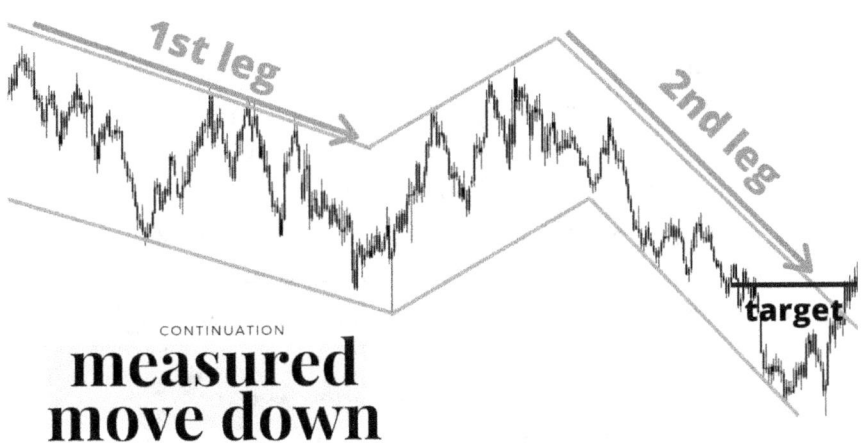

- The measured move down chart pattern has three parts. It can begin as a reversal pattern in an uptrend, then go into a range before a final reversal pattern of the original uptrend.

- The bearish measured move down pattern can't be identified until *after* the first correction and breakdown of the consolidation phase.
- The first leg of decline usually starts around the lows of the previous uptrend and may start trending down for a few weeks or months.
- After the initial downtrend, a consolidation or correction is the next phase in this pattern. If it is a consolidation, there could be a trading range such as a rectangle or descending triangle before the next leg to the downside.
- If this pattern follows through as a reversal, there could be a 50% decline on the next leg down. The equivalent magnitude of the previous decline and the possible consolidation pattern could look like a descending rectangle price channel.
- The length from high to low of the first leg of the downtrend can be used on the low of the consolidation range to project a profit target on the continuation of the downtrend.
- If the bearish measured move pattern forms and the consolidation or correction phase evolves into a continuation pattern, then entry points for the next phase of the downtrend can be signaled using the breakdown of the support line in the consolidation pattern.
- This is typically a long-term chart and forms over many months.
- The measured move is a continuation pattern.
- Volume increases at the beginning of the initial reversal into a downtrend. It decreases as the consolidation comes to an end. Beginning to increase again with a breakdown to confirm the continuation of the downtrend increases this pattern's odds of success.

This Schlumberger chart shows the reversal of an uptrend into a downtrend off a high near $49. The first leg of the downtrend was from April through May 2019 and created a descending price channel. After a May 31, 2019 low in price of $34.46, a new uptrending price channel emerged on the chart from June to mid-July and peaked at $41.40. The second leg down in price began in mid-July and lasted until the end of August of 2019. The descending upper trendlines were finally broken and the chart evolved into an uptrend. This pattern is an example of how long-term downtrends don't always go straight down. They can be interrupted by trading ranges and swings back higher to the upside before resuming a big downtrend.

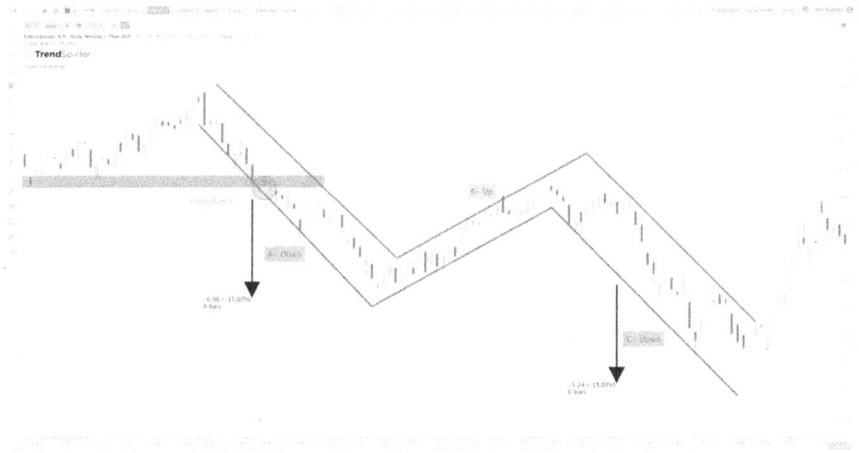

Chart by Jake Wujastyk at TrendSpider.com

Summary

The bearish measured move down is a three phase chart pattern that includes an initial strong downtrend coming after a trading range or bull market. The next phase starts as the downtrend stalls and consolidates in an ascending rectangle price channel. The continuation of the downtrend is confirmed as the consolidation phase is broken out of to the downside and the downtrend resumes. The magnitude of the move down out of the consolidation phase can be half the size or as large as the initial downtrend.

17

DESCENDING SCALLOP

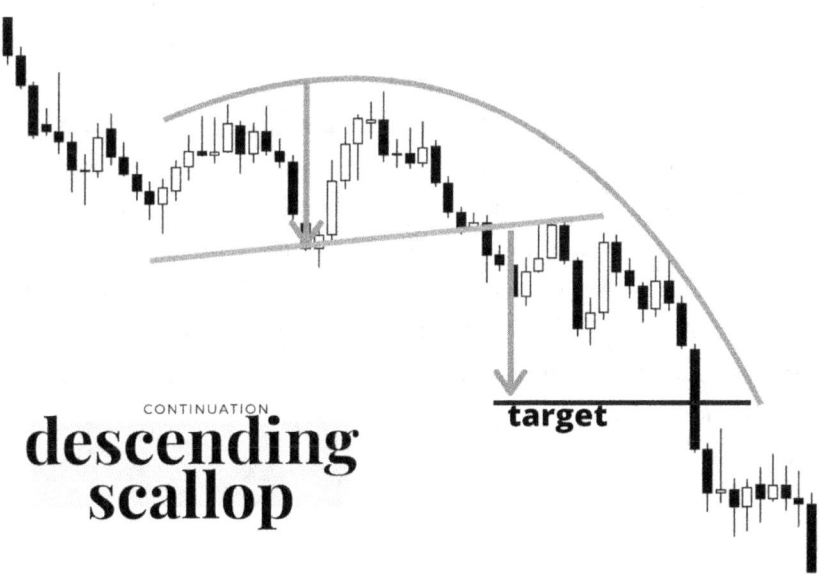

- The descending scallop is a bearish reversal pattern.
- Descending scallops are common topping chart patterns.
- This is a downward trending chart pattern.
- This chart pattern curves like an inverted letter *J*. The

descending scallop is formed by two lows in price on each side and a rounded price resistance range in-between the lower price valleys.
- Descending scallops sometimes show inverted U-shaped volume as the topping pattern forms.
- They generally don't follow through lower when the market itself is in a long-term uptrend.
- The descending scallop price range is wider near the start and the finish of the pattern of the curved top.
- Breakouts to the upside of the descending scallop chart pattern can invalidate the bearish bias and lead to quick rises in price after a breakout to the upside.

This Marathon oil chart shows the descending scallop pattern before the pandemic and oil price crash of 2020. It continued to make lower highs and lower lows throughout February, before going into a short-term range and creating the curved resistance topping pattern. After the chart had a breakdown under the support in the scallop, it experienced a large gap down in price and went into a volatile trading range. This is a good example of a company that is tied very closely to the price of one commodity. Its chart is vulnerable to a crash if a panic over price sweeps through the markets. Chart patterns are a good filter for technical price action that can warn traders about gap downs and downtrends, regardless of the historical fundamental value of a company's commodity.

THE ULTIMATE GUIDE TO CHART PATTERNS

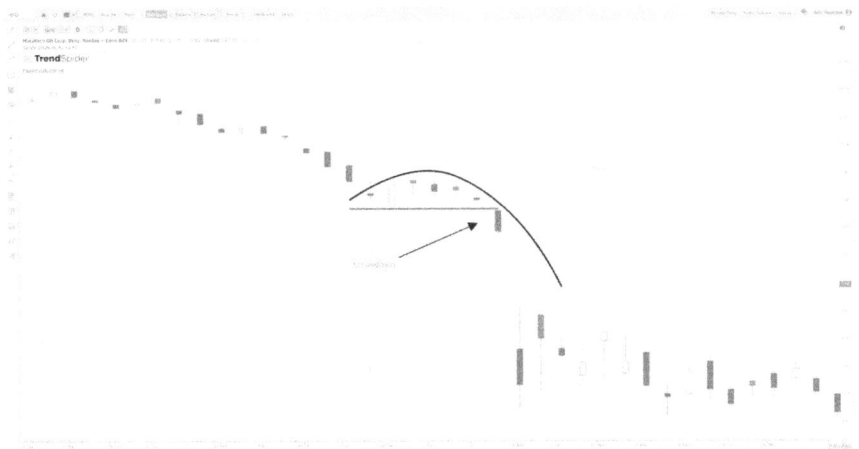

Chart by Jake Wujastyk at TrendSpider.com

Summary

The descending scallop is a bearish topping consolidation chart pattern and similar to the inverted *cup* in the inverted cup with handle chart pattern. However, an ideal scallop pattern is wider and more round. It consists of higher highs and higher lows on the left side of the scallop, and lower highs and lower lows on the right side that create an inverted, curved scallop shape. The bearish sell short signal is a breakdown of the horizontal line of support at the low of the scallop pattern. The old low can be new resistance if a downtrend begins. A close below the lowest price in the pattern signals a breakout to the downside. A stop loss can be set with a close above the low of the pattern.

18

THREE FALLING PEAKS

- The three falling peaks is a chart pattern that forms with swings in price at the end of a long term uptrend.
- The three falling peaks of resistance qualify as a bearish

pattern. The three peaks and two valleys in price should be similar in size and magnitude.
- This chart pattern can be a good performer for short selling at the end of bull markets. It's caused by lower swings in the trading range before an uptrend goes into a major pullback or correction.
- It triggers a sell short signal as a valid breakdown of this chart pattern, when price closes below the lowest valley in the pattern on the third attempt, after the third low in price support doesn't hold.
- Each swing in price from up and back down must create a lower low. This pattern confirms and can signal a trend change and reversal of an uptrend when three lower lows appear.
- The chart gives a momentum reversal trend signal after the low of the two support levels in the pattern is broken to the downside.
- This pattern can appear on different time frames.
- This is usually a bearish reversal pattern.
- The three falling peaks in this pattern are created when three rallies in price fail to make a higher high each time. The lows in this pattern are created by two lower lows for support levels creating two *valleys* that must be a lower low than the previous one.
- Each of the three peaks and two valleys should be very close to the same depth, size and duration. Don't use irregular peaks and valleys when looking for this pattern.
- This chart pattern confirms a momentum short sell signal when price closes below the lowest valley in the two valley section of the pattern.
- This pattern gives better odds of a winning trade when increased volume follows the trend through the breakdown of support.

- The bigger the uptrend is and the more overbought the market is leading up to this pattern's breakdown, the better the risk/reward ratio is skewed in a short seller's favor.
- Another potential entry point is to sell short on a reversal of the third lower peak. This entry has a lower probability of success because the pattern has not fully formed. An early entry can give you a better risk/reward ratio if the pattern follows through to the downside.
- This pattern is better as a short selling signal than a long position stop loss because the path of least resistance is down.

This Marathon oil chart illustrates this pattern by showing how it made three lower highs and had swings in price back to a lower price peak after each pullback into a valley of support. Both the second valley and third valley made a lower low than the previous valley. After the third peak with a lower high, the third pullback lost the previous valley support and the chart fell into a downtrend.

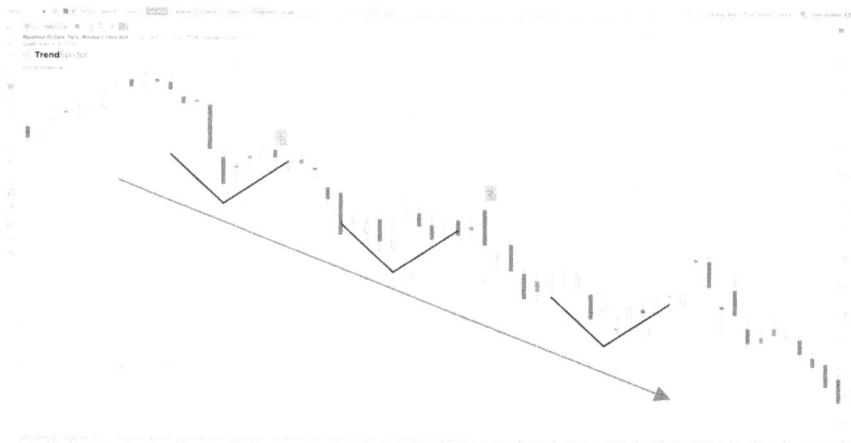

Chart by Jake Wujastyk at TrendSpider.com

Summary

This is a bearish pattern defined by three similar moves in magnitude, each having a lower low than the previous one. The low valley in price between the second and third peak in price, should be lower than the low price valley between the first and second high in price of the peaks. The big picture for this pattern is that there are three lower highs in price and two lower lows. The third lower low is the signal in price to sell short in the hopes of capturing the beginning of a downtrend.

19

RISING WEDGE

- The rising wedge chart pattern can fit in the continuation or reversal category. When it's a continuation pattern it will trend up, but the slope in the wedge will be against the overall market downtrend. When it's a reversal

pattern, the rising wedge trends up when the overall market is in an uptrend.
- The rising wedge is a bearish pattern regardless of what kind of market it's in.
- The rising wedge is a bearish chart pattern that begins with a wide trading range at the bottom, and contracts to a smaller trading range as prices trend up.
- This price action forms an ascending cone shape that trends higher as the vertical highs and vertical lows move towards a convergence.
- The bearish bias in this pattern can't be signaled until a breakdown of the ascending support shows it as a reversal pattern from highs in price.
- This long-term pattern generally forms over a one to six month time frame.
- The new highs set in this pattern create higher highs, but the new highs should have less magnitude. Less strength in highs indicates a decrease in the strength of buying pressure. It should create an upper trendline of resistance with less ascending slope than the lower line of support.

This Advanced Micro Devices chart shows a rising wedge forming in January following an upswing in price. It had a sharp breakdown in the ascending lower support line and a fast downswing in price before continuing its sharp move to the upside.

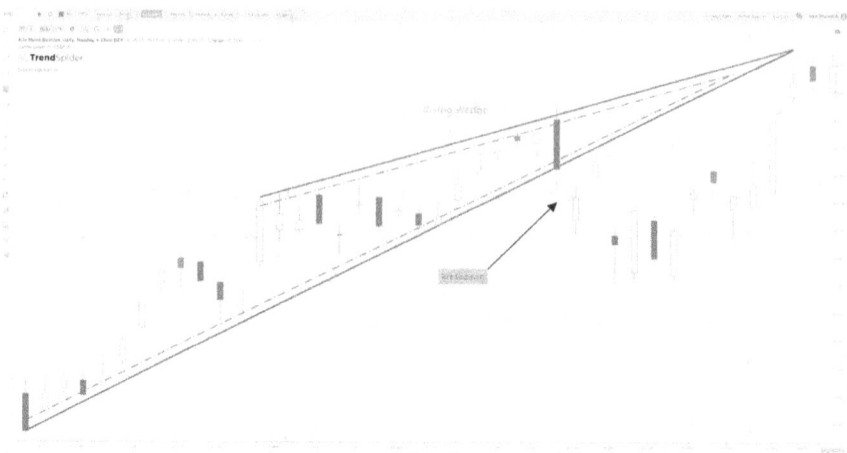

Chart by Jake Wujastyk at TrendSpider.com

Summary

The rising wedge is a long-term bearish chart pattern that has an ascending line of resistance and an ascending line of support. The resistance line should lose strength and trend higher with less magnitude as the pattern forms, which shows that buying pressure is decreasing. If the ascending line of support is broken to the downside as the lines converge, this pattern is either a continuation of a downtrend if it's a bear market, or a reversal from a near term price top if the pattern forms during a bull market.

NEUTRAL PATTERNS

20

SYMMETRICAL TRIANGLES

- The symmetrical triangle is a neutral chart pattern that typically forms during a trend as a continuation pattern of the existing trend.
- A symmetrical triangle pattern may form as a reversal

pattern as a trend comes to an end, but they are typically a continuation patterns of an existing trend.
- The symmetrical triangle takes shape when the descending and ascending trendlines converge.
- A symmetrical triangle has a wide trading range at the beginning of the pattern, and compresses to a very small range as the pattern plays out.
- The symmetrical pattern creates a coil, and contains at least two lower highs and two higher lows for a compression of the price range into an apex point.
- The lower highs is a sign of buyers losing interest in higher prices. Higher lows show that sellers are not letting their position go at lower prices. The pattern makes higher lows at the same time it makes lower highs.
- The top descending resistance line on this pattern trends downward at the same time that the lower support line trends up with higher lows.
- While similar to the pennant pattern, the symmetrical triangle patterns can be longer in time frame and wider in range.
- Volume will often contract as the pattern gets close to its apex. A breakout with higher than average volume can be a successful buy signal.
- As a symmetrical triangle contracts and the price range shrinks, volume should start to decline. This can be a compression in price action before a breakout.
- The price target projection for this pattern after the breakout is typically found by measuring the longest distance in the price range of the pattern, and projecting after the resistance breakout.

This Tesla chart shows a symmetrical triangle after a two and a half month trading range. This triangle could have broken either way, but the breakout near the apex as the two trendlines met went up and followed through for an uptrend from the breakout of the descending upper trendlines. The high of the triangle was near $500 at its peak, and the low was near $335 as the trading range contracted until one side broke out.

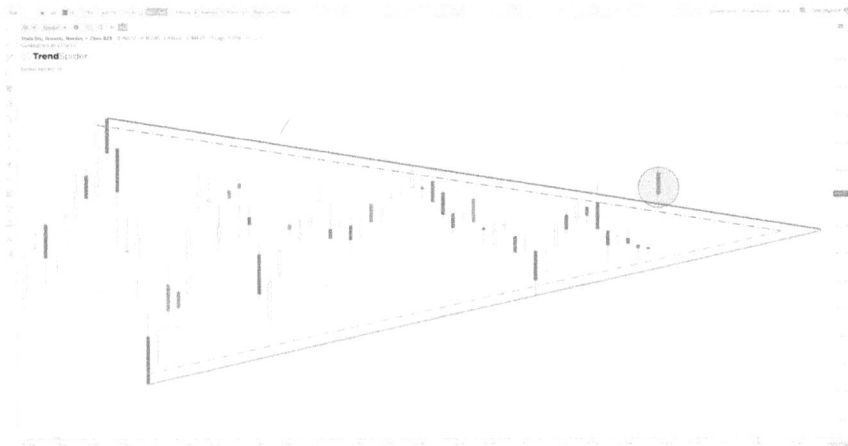

Chart by Jake Wujastyk at TrendSpider.com

This JP Morgan chart shows a symmetrical triangle after a three and a half month trading range. This triangle could have broken either way but the breakout near the apex as the two trendliness met was down and followed through for a downswing from the break of the ascending lower trendline. The high of the triangle was near $116 at its peak and the low was near $91, as the trading range contracted until the downside finally broke.

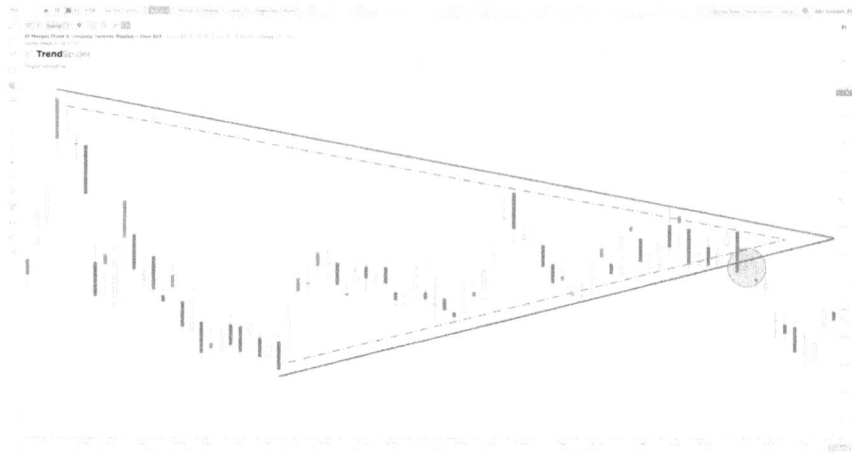

Chart by Jake Wujastyk at TrendSpider.com

Summary

The symmetrical triangle is a neutral chart pattern with resistance at the top descending vertical trendline that makes lower highs, and support at the ascending vertical trendline that makes higher lows. A breakout of the descending trendline near the apex of the converging trendlines is the signal that can either be a bullish or bearish entry signal, based on the direction of the breakout. A stop loss could be set if price returns and closes on the other side of the apex of trendline convergence. The gain if the pattern breaks and trends could be equal to the size of the largest area of the trading range inside the pattern. A price target could be for a run after the breakout equal to the largest point of the trading range inside the triangle.

REVERSAL PATTERNS

21

HEAD & SHOULDERS

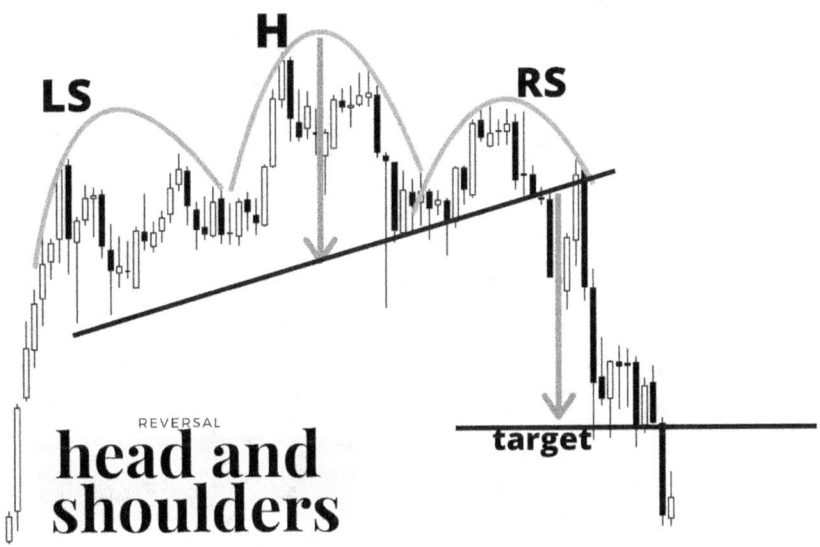

- The head and shoulders chart pattern is a reversal pattern of an uptrend. The pattern is formed during a bull market or a chart in an uptrend. The completion of this pattern is bearish and is typically a setup for a pullback, correction or bear market. A previous uptrend must be in place before this pattern can be considered valid.

- This pattern consists of three peaks with the middle, higher peak creating the *head* and each smaller peak is a *shoulder*. The low of support that creates the valleys between the peaks is used to create the *neckline, the* horizontal support.
- The break of the neckline support to the downside is the signal line to sell or sell short.
- The left shoulder is created during the first upswing in the uptrend. Price then pulls back to support on the downswing.
- The next upswing in price goes higher than the left shoulder and breaks out to a new higher high. It eventually swings lower to near the previous low price of support.
- The third upswing in price is lower than the middle peak that is the *head* and similar in size to the first high in price that is the left shoulder. Price then swings back lower for the third time near the previous two areas of support.
- The three swing backs to low price support should be similar to create a horizontal support line that is the neckline in this pattern. This line can be very flat or trend up or down. A neckline that is trending down is another indicator of the end of the uptrend.
- This pattern should see declining volume to the upside of the head and shoulders and increasing volume as it swings lower after each peak to give additional signs of distribution.
- The head and shoulders pattern is not confirmed until the neckline of the pattern is broken. Many times the old support at the neckline becomes the new resistance as price tries to rally back up after the break down.

Increasing volume on the break below the neckline is more confirmation of the potential for a downtrend.
- The magnitude of the move down can many times be the same magnitude as the distance from the neckline to the top of the head in the head and shoulders pattern.

The below Boeing weekly chart shows a head and shoulders pattern that took over two years to play out. The left and right shoulders are similar in size but smaller than the head. The neckline support is measured from left to right at the first low after the left shoulder. Additional signs of a reversal were the large bearish candlesticks after each failure for price to go higher throughout the pattern formation. Price initially held the lower neckline support and rallied back four times over two years before finally breaking down strongly in March 2020. A close below the neckline was the sell short signal in this pattern with a stop loss could have been set on a rally back over this line. Notice that the move from the neckline to the peak of the head and the move from the neckline to the bottom of the downtrend was similar in magnitude. Sometimes it takes multiple entries at breakdowns and stop losses being hit before catching the big down move that pays for all the false signals, patience pays.

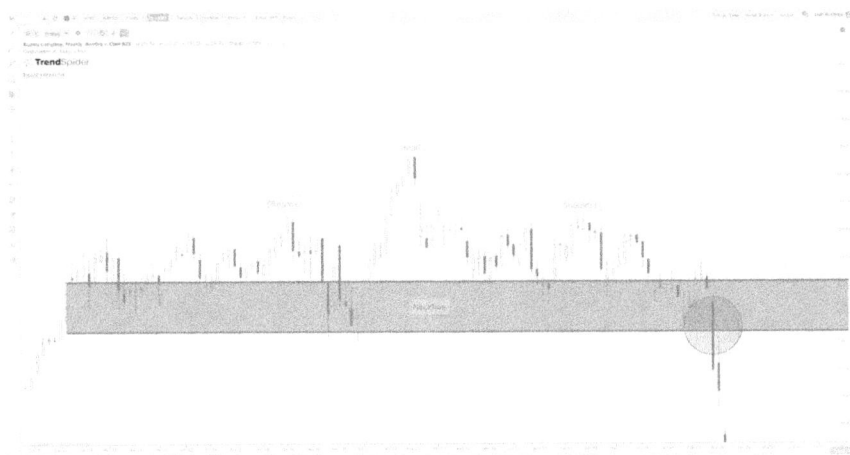

Chart by Jake Wujastyk at TrendSpider.com

Summary

This pattern is created at the end of a bull market in a chart when the market exhausts buyers and each of three highs in price is met with selling pressure through profit taking. The head of the pattern generally creates a market top. The support line of the neck is where buyers step in with volume to rally price up on sellers two times but not the third. The pattern can be irregular in sizes and shapes; the key is seeing the three peaks with the middle higher than the other two that are similar in size and the middle line of support close to each pullback.

22

INVERTED HEAD AND SHOULDERS

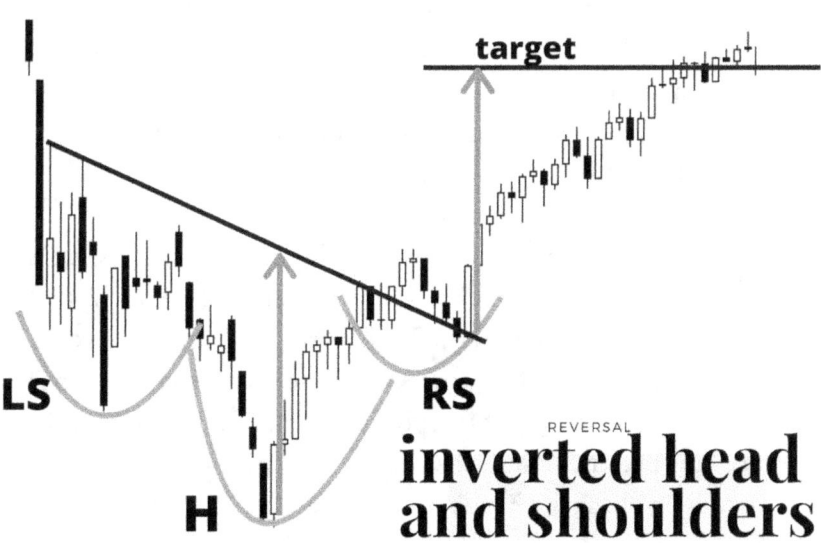

- This pattern is called the reverse or inverse head and shoulders chart pattern or a head and shoulders bottom, and is a reversal pattern in a downtrend. The pattern is formed during a bear market or downtrend. The completion of this pattern is bullish and is usually a setup for a new uptrend at the beginning of a bull market. A previous downtrend must be in place before this pattern can be considered valid.

- This pattern may form near a bottom in a downtrend.
- This pattern consists of three valleys with a much lower middle valley that creates the *head* and each smaller valley creates a *shoulder*. The high for the peaks between the valleys is used to create the horizontal or vertical resistance which is the *neckline*.
- The signal to buy is the breakout of the neckline resistance to the upside.
- The left shoulder is created during the first downswing. Price then pulls back to resistance on the upswing.
- The next downswing in price goes lower than the left shoulder and breaks down to a new lower low. It eventually swings back up to near the previous resistance high in price.
- The next downswing in price goes lower than the left shoulder to a new low, but swings back up to near the previous resistance high in price.
- The three swings back to the high price resistance should be similar to create a horizontal resistance line that is the neckline in this pattern. This resistance line can be very flat or trend up or down. A neckline that is trending up is another indicator of the potential end of the downtrend.
- This pattern should see declining volume to the downside of the head and shoulders, and increasing volume as it swings higher after each valley. This gives additional signs of accumulation and buying of the dips in price.
- The inverse head and shoulders patterns are not confirmed until the neckline of the pattern is broken to the upside. The old resistance at the neckline often

becomes the new support as price pulls back after the breakout to the upside. Increasing volume on the break above the neckline is more confirmation of the potential for a new uptrend.
- The magnitude of the move up can be the same magnitude as the distance from the neckline to the bottom of the head in this inverted pattern.

This Nvidia chart shows an inverse head and shoulders pattern forming for three months between two upswings in price. The head is lower than both shoulders with the right shoulder being lower than the left shoulder and the neckline descending. There were several powerful bullish candlesticks and two gap ups in price that attempted to breakout of the neckline and trigger long signals until price finally rallied higher. This was a bottoming pattern that indicated a new uptrend starting, with the momentum signal of the breakout that followed through for the next leg of the uptrend.

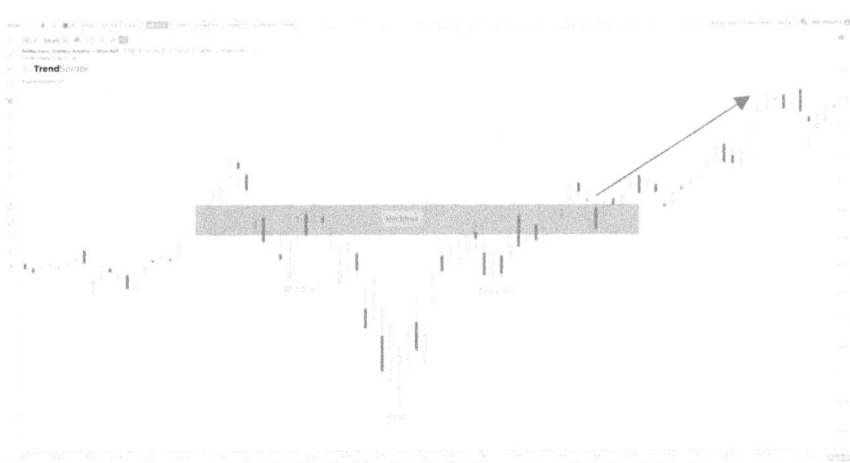

Chart by Jake Wujastyk at TrendSpider.com

Summary

The inverse head and shoulders pattern is created at the end of a bear market when the market exhausts sellers and each of three lows in price is met with new buying pressure and short covering. The head of the pattern generally creates a market bottom. The resistance line of the neck acts as resistance as prices go lower twice, but the third time lows hold near the first shoulder support. The pattern can be irregular in size and shape. The key is seeing the three valleys with the middle much lower than the other two.

23

DOUBLE BOTTOMS

The double bottom pattern is a bullish reversal pattern. This pattern is created when a key price support level on a chart is tested twice, with a rally between the two support level tests.

- A double bottom chart pattern happens at the end of a downtrend that has likely gone on for weeks or months.
- The first bounce off support where price stops falling is the first support level.
- The first bounce and reversal in the downtrend is small, and the short-term run up is usually approximately 5% to 10% off the support lows.
- The first rally off the lows fails and price returns to the previous support.
- The previous price support lows hold on the second test.
- The second test of support must be confirmed by a reversal and trend. It's only a potential pattern until support holds and price rallies off the support with higher volume, and sometimes a gap up in price.
- A breakout back over the high price that occurred in the middle between the double bottom support tests, is a full confirmation of the double bottom reversal pattern. This is the level that can signal a long entry.
- A double bottom chart pattern can take weeks and even months to play out, with the middle
rally resistance taking many different sizes and shapes.

On this Exxon Mobil chart example, the double bottom support level is the horizontal support zone between $33 and $30. One potential buy signal for this chart was a bounce off the double bottom support near $29, and a break back out of the double bottom support zone around $33.

THE ULTIMATE GUIDE TO CHART PATTERNS 91

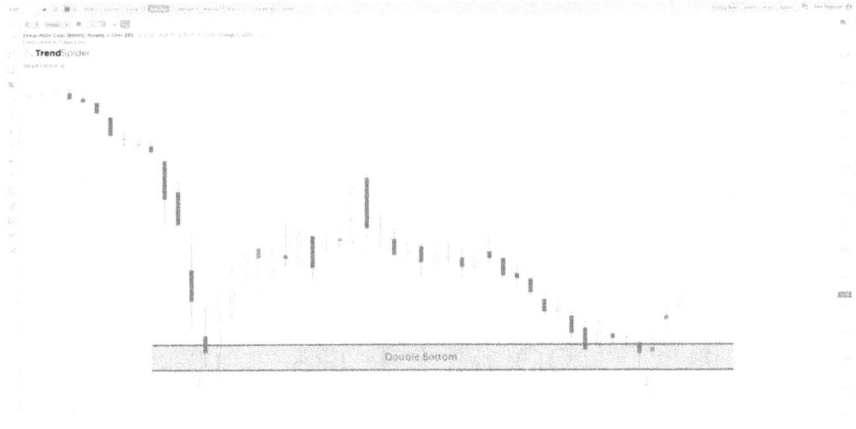

Chart by Jake Wujastyk at TrendSpider.com

Summary

This pattern is one way to locate high probability dip buys after an extended downtrend in price. It also gives you a way to quantify your stop loss. If you choose to take the dip buy off the second support level, your stop would be a close below the first price level of support. If you buy a trendline breakout of the middle-line of resistance, then the stop loss can be set with a break back under the middle resistance line. This chart pattern shows buyers located near the same price zone twice revealing demand on the chart.

24

DOUBLE TOPS

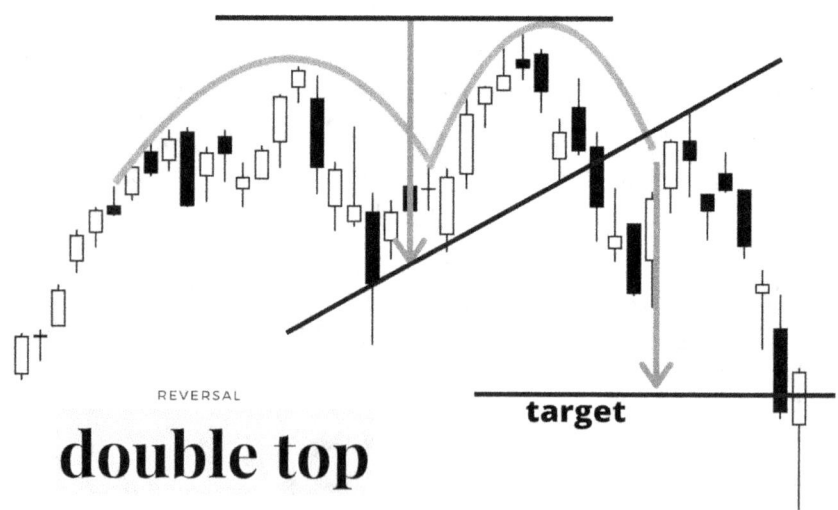

The double top chart is a bearish reversal pattern. This pattern is created when a key price resistance level on a chart is tested twice, and a pullback between the two high prices creates a price support level zone.

- A double top chart pattern happens near the end of an uptrend that has likely gone on for weeks or months.
- The first bounce off resistance where price stops going up is the first level of price resistance.
- The first rejection and reversal in the uptrend is small and the short-term pullback is usually about 5% to 10% off the resistance highs.
- The first pullback from the highs bounces in a support zone, and later price returns to close at the previous resistance zone. However, it's usually a little lower than the previous high price.
- The previous price resistance highs hold on the second test.
- The second test of resistance must be confirmed by a reversal and pullback to support between the two peaks. This is only a potential pattern until price resistance holds and price is rejected off the previous high price area, with higher volume and sometimes a large bearish candlestick or a gap down in price.
- If there is a close in price above the previous high, the double top is invalidated and the odds are that the uptrend continues.
- A break under the low price that occurred in the middle between the double top resistance levels is a full confirmation momentum signal of the double top reversal pattern. This is the level where a signal to sell or sell short is given.
- Selling short at a higher price after the rejection of resistance at the second top has lower odds of success, but it has a better risk/reward ratio.
- A double top chart pattern can take weeks or months to play out, and the middle pullback to support can have many different sizes and shapes.

This is an example of the double top pattern on the Marathon oil weekly chart before a sell-off to the downside. The first price top failed to break above resistance after three attempts in late July and early August. It failed to break out higher on two attempts in late November. The neckline of the pattern didn't break down and provided support as the chart began to go sideways. In this example, the old support between the double tops became the same support zone in the new trading range after the double top pattern.

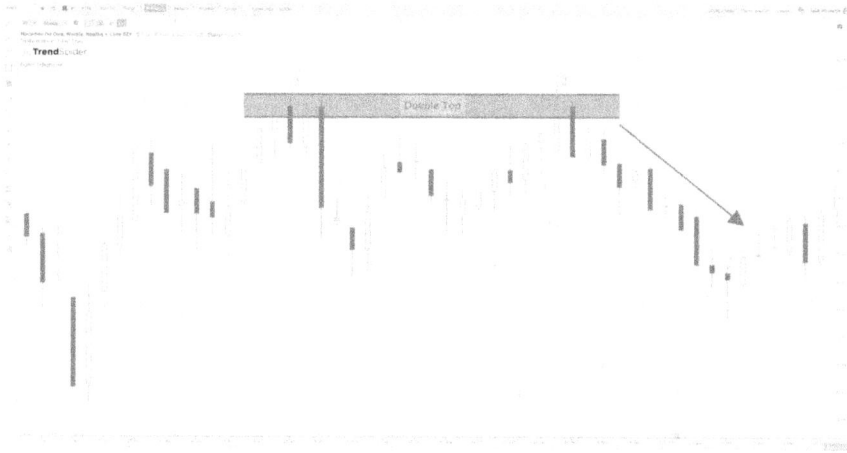

Chart by Jake Wujastyk at TrendSpider.com

Summary

This pattern is one way to locate high probability short selling opportunities after an extended uptrend in price. It also gives you a way to quantify your stop loss. If you choose to take the short sell off the second resistance level, your stop would be a close above the first price level of resistance. If you short sell a trendline breakdown of the middle line of support, then the stop loss can be set with a break back above the middle support line. A double top pattern can be followed by a downtrend or a trading range.

RAINDROP CHART PATTERNS

Throughout this book we've used candlestick charts in our examples with both templates and historical chart patterns. In this chapter, Ruslan Lagutin from TrendSpider.com is going to discuss their new raindrop charts. He'll explain how they're different from candlesticks and how they add volume into each price chart.

RAINDROP CHARTS ARE A NEW KIND OF FINANCIAL CHART designed to let you see what is happening in the market from a unique perspective. Raindrops are built from the same market data as Japanese candlesticks, but incorporate volume into the final visualization, showing you how price and volume play out over time.

The left side of a Raindrop represents the first half of the period and the right side represents the second half of the period. Each half is essentially a small Volume at Price, or Volume Profile, chart (that has been rotated 90 degrees). This lets you see how market sentiment changes by comparing the first half of each period's histogram to the second half's histogram.

The "Raindrop" Chart Explained

THE BEST WAY TO SEE THE BENEFITS OF RAINDROP CHARTS OVER conventional Japanese candlestick charts is to look at an example. In this image, the 30 minute center Raindrop (blue circle, marked B – long green one in the middle) tells a much more comprehensive story about volume and price action than the corresponding 30 minute candlestick (red circle, marked B).

Let's dig into that for a moment with the image below.

- **The Japanese Candle (B):** The price has moved upwards. There's no lower wick, means that price never went lower than open, which probably indicates a strong base and price movement.
- **The Raindrop (B):** The price has moved upwards. There was nearly no volume behind lower 70% of the Drop's price range; all the real trading was happening in the upper 30%. During the first 15 minutes, volume was half of what it was during the last 15 minutes, which probably means that the market was pretty sure about the price level as soon as it has reached it.
- Now, to dive deeper, compare this Raindrop visualization to the 5 minute Candles on the left (which show a more granular story), and you will see that the

30 minute Raindrops provide a high degree of granularity, even at higher time frames. Now let's take a bigger chart and demonstrate the real power of Raindrop charts.

Comparison: Raindrops vs. Candles on ADSK

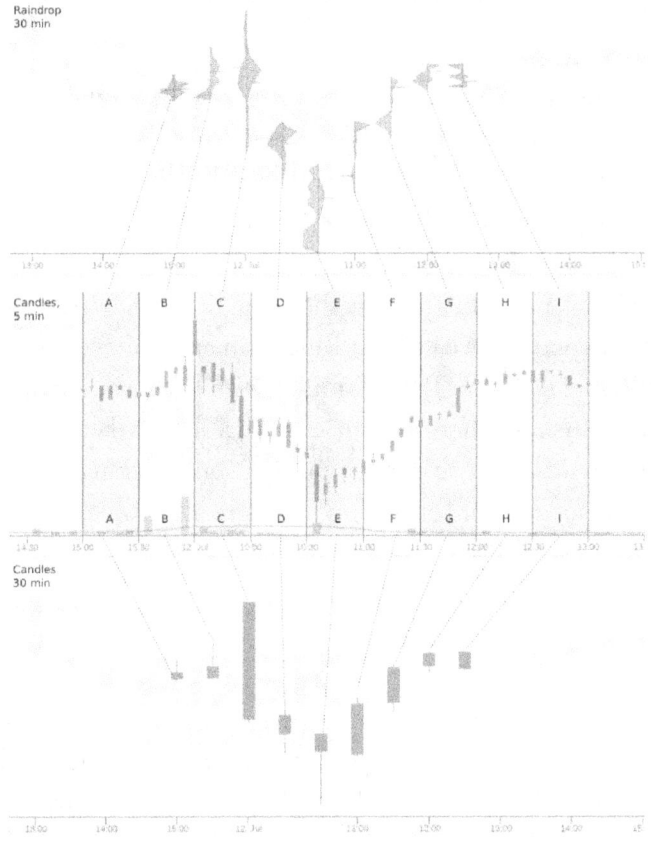

The key difference between raindrops and candles is that candles are constructed using traditional open and close prices, which I perceive as random price breaks: set by the passage of time, and containing no unique information about the price other than its timestamp. Conversely, raindrops use left and right volume-weighted average prices (VWAPs) instead, which contain a deeper level of information about movements in more than just price — it shows the sentiment of a market.

In the above illustration, you can see a clear difference at candle E, but let's walk through them one by one.

Period A

- 30 Minute Candlestick
- Smaller red body, mediocre upside wick and short lower one. Candle's range is rather usual (see the candles on the left).
- Conclusion: Price has moved down a little bit.
- 30 Minute Raindrop
- Volume-weighted price is the same through both halves of the period. We call it a Blue Doji and believe it reflects a "True Doji" for those familiar with the term.
- Conclusion: There's a consensus on the market, and things are likely to change pretty soon. We have observed these forming at future support or resistance levels, or before volatility.

Period B

- 30 Minute Candlestick
- Price has moved up but closed at like 50% of a range. It might even be a Bullish Engulfing, should this low be slightly lower.
- 30 Minute Raindrop
- Price has moved upwards significantly, but on the second half of the period there was no clear consensus about the market price: Nearly the same volume was traded on top of range and on the lower 40% of the range.

Period C

- 30 Minute Candlestick
- All hell broke loose. We have started high and ended low, candle has nearly no wicks. That's a good and bold bearish engulfing.
- Conclusion: Market was bold with the movement.
- 30 Minute Raindrop
- Price range was wide, but all the real stuff was happening mostly in the middle of this range, through both halves of the period.
- Conclusion: Market was not quite sure if it goes down or not.

Period D

- 30 Minute Candlestick
- Just a red candle, with wicks being probably slightly longer than usual.
- 30 Minute Raindrop
- During both halves of the period, most of the volume was traded in the upper 50% of a price range. Left and right prices are nearly the same. This drop was close to becoming a blue doji.

Period E

- 30 Minute Candlestick
- This is a hammer. Reversal is likely to happen (in 60% of cases, based on studies).
- Conclusion: Reversal is likely to happen.
- 30 Minute Raindrop
- During the first half of the period, the market was very

unsure about the price. But during the second half, most volume was traded in upper 50% of a range.
- Conclusion: This is a reversal, at least a short-term one.

Period F

- 30 Minute Candlestick
- Bearish 3-line strike + bullish engulfing. bullish reversal is likely (84% chance). The price obviously went up.
- Conclusion: Market moves higher, the movement seems to be strong.
- 30 Minute Raindrop
- Market moved higher. The dominating volume was traded during the second half of the period, and it was in the top 10% of the period.
- Conclusion: Market was eager to go upwards, it was a bold movement.

Period G

- 30 Minute Candlestick
- Still moving up, forming a new maximum.
- 30 Minute Raindrop
- Market moved up even more. But during the second half of the period, almost two times less volume traded compared to the first half.
- Conclusion: The market moved higher but might lose future momentum.

Period H

- 30 Minute Candlestick
- Price still moves up. Candles' range obviously narrows down; might be a sign of losing momentum.

- 30 Minute Raindrop
- In general, the same story as on drop G, but price range has narrowed down. Market still loses the inertia.

Period I

- 30 Minute Candlestick
- Bearish Engulfing, we're likely to go down.
- 30 Minute Raindrop
- Huge uncertainty during first half of period (take a look at these 3 peaks on VbP chart!). Market has come to consensus during second half, and this consensus price is in the lowest 20% of a drop's price range. But this consensus is not looking bold, given that summary volume during second half was like 2x lower than for the first half.

Key Takeaways

MANY OF THE TRADITIONAL CANDLESTICKS FORM PATTERNS. To get the most out of candlestick charts, it is helpful to have an understanding of these common historical candlestick patterns that show market turning points.

With the Raindrops, the charts are naturally intuitive. You need nothing but common sense to see the market flowing from one point of balance to another. It is clearly visualized with the volume histograms.

Raindrops tell simple yet informative stories. You don't need to memorize patterns or complex rules in order to understand them. Raindrops give you a much deeper look into the market's sentiment flow, while still maintaining low amounts of noise.

Below are four charts created by Jake Wujastyk at TrendSpider.com that show the differences between traditional candlestick charts and using volume weighted raindrop charts to identify chart patterns.

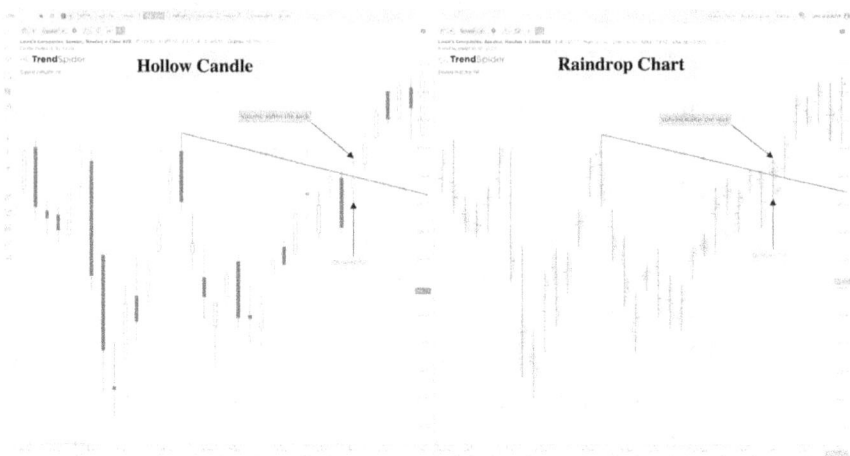

Chart by Jake Wujastyk at TrendSpider.com

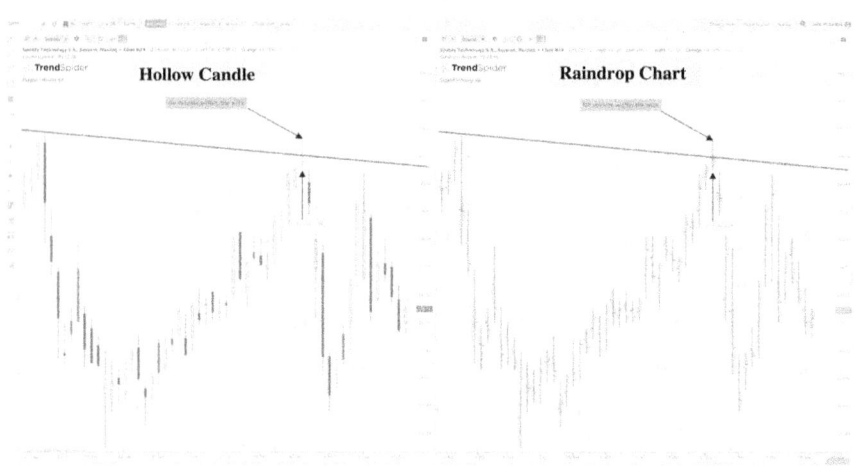

Chart by Jake Wujastyk at TrendSpider.com

THE ULTIMATE GUIDE TO CHART PATTERNS   103

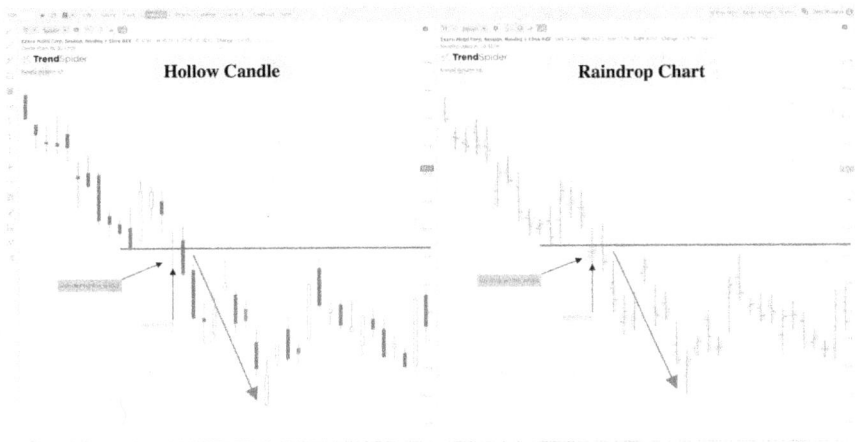

Chart by Jake Wujastyk at TrendSpider.com

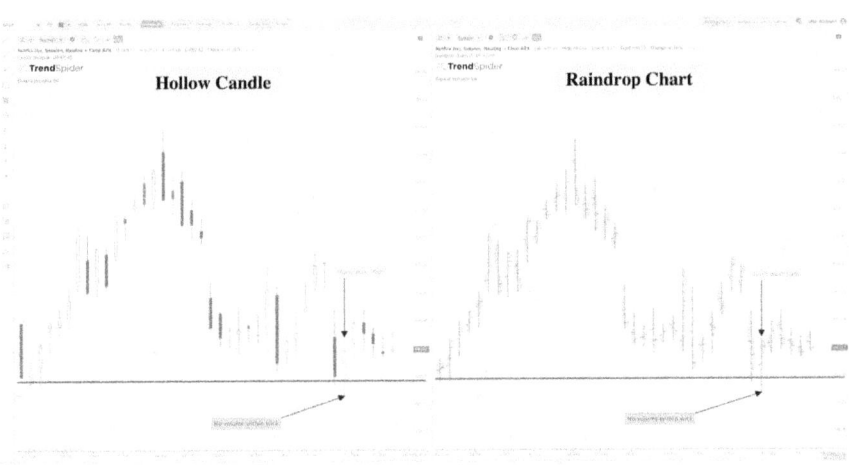

Chart by Jake Wujastyk at TrendSpider.com

Summary

Raindrop charts are an interesting technical tool that you may want to consider using when studying chart patterns, because they add the dynamics of volume inside each time period bar. They can help with evaluating trendlines, price resistance and support zones.

CONCLUSION

Entries

- Most chart pattern signals are a trendline break in the direction of the trend that the pattern is pointing to. Most chart pattern entries will be momentum signals in the direction of the prevalent trend or a reversal of the current trend.
- Wait for your signal to be triggered before entering a trade. Don't attempt to front run an entry and anticipate that something will happen. One edge in trading chart patterns is that traders exchange their opinions and predictions for signals. They trade in the path of least resistance.
- While chart patterns can play out on any time frame, waiting for end of day signals before entering increases the odds of success for swing and trend trades. An end of day strategy ensures confirmation of the entry on the daily chart at close.
- Don't chase a trade if you miss a signal after it has

become extended. Late entries skew your risk/reward ratio. If you miss the first breakout, it's better to wait for a pullback to the signal area for a second chance entry.
- You don't have to recover trading losses on the same chart you lost money on. A large watchlist helps you identify chart patterns that are setting up for better entries. The best time to trade chart patterns is in a trend with momentum.
- Always enter based on a trading plan and not greed or emotion. Emotions are dangerous advisors when you let them influence your position sizing and stop loss placement.

Exits

- An initial stop loss can be set for a close against your position on the other side of your entry signal. For a long position, a close below your entry trendline break. For a short sell, a close back above your entry trendline. This initial stop loss will define your risk, while an initial profit target can show the potential for reward. The combination of the two will give you your risk/reward ratio on entry.
- If the trade doesn't trend in your favor and price breaks the pattern formation that you were looking for, it's better to take a small loss early. When the pattern you were trading is invalidated by price action, get out and look for better trading opportunities with other patterns.
- It's crucial that you let a winning trade run as far as you can to maximize gains. Initial profit targets should be set for a move in the magnitude of the previous trend or range in the pattern. Your initial profit will define your potential reward on entry.
- Trailing stops can be used to let a winner run. A trailing

stop can be a close below the previous day's low, a short term moving average like the 10-day EMA or a technical signal like MACD. Each chart is different so the dynamics will vary.
- Be flexible in your trade management as a trade goes in your favor. Draw trendlines daily and look for the big picture in the trend. If the market continues to make higher highs let a long position run. If the market continues to make lower lows let a short position run.

Chart pattern trading tips

- Develop a watch list of markets/stocks that tend to trend historically. Review them daily for any chart patterns that develop. Energy, tech, metals and growth stocks are some of the best markets for trends and patterns.
- Chart pattern trading has to be done inside a well-developed trading plan. It should define position sizing, maximum risk exposure, chosen markets, time frame, frequency and goals for maximum drawdown and your goals for capital returns.
- Any trading system you choose to implement must have an edge, fit your own risk tolerance and have the potential to meet your return goals. *Then you must trade it with discipline long enough to let the edge play out.*
- Chart patterns are not the Holy Grail of trading. Some chart patterns play out as trends after their breakouts, and others fade back inside the pattern and don't trend. Profitably trading chart patterns comes from creating a good risk/reward ratio. This is created by placing a stop loss that is set when the pattern is invalidated for a small loss, and a reward is maximized by letting a winner run for a large gain.
- Establish clear rules for trading chart patterns and follow

them with discipline. There is no way to trade profitably long-term without discipline. Consistency is needed to make money trading chart patterns.

- Focus on the process or trading your system and not the results you get from a single trade. Different patterns will lead to different results. You need a large sample of trades over the long-term to let your trading results play out. A few big trends can make your whole year.
- Lower your risk of making errors due to stress by trading with a position size that is comfortable for you mentally and emotionally. Each trade should be just one of the next one hundred trades. It shouldn't lead to excessive financial risk or stress because you fear a large drawdown.
- A trading journal with annotated charts and your past trades can help you identify what you are good at and what you need to work on. This journal, if kept diligently, will highlight your strengths, weaknesses, and why you make certain errors.
- A chart pattern is a visual tool to see where buyers and sellers are agreeing in price and the overall trend of the market. You trade chart patterns when there is a signal that a change in price agreement has begun which could determine the next direction in price trend.

Understanding chart patterns can be a useful technical tool for a trader. It allows you to see the reality of the trend in a market, regardless of personal opinions or predictions. A chart pattern is a visual map of where the buyers and sellers are making the decisions on where to get in and out. Traders and investors leave their clues behind for the next market move, and finding those clues is what the technical analysis of chart patterns is all about.

ACKNOWLEDGMENTS

Jake Wujastyk of TrendSpider.com used their excellent trading platform to create the historical chart images in this book. We're big fans of TrendSpider and recommend them to our students. Here are a few reasons we think their software is pretty great:

- Benzinga News Feed included (usually something that you have to buy)
- Analyst ratings
- Seasonality
- Anchored VWAP/Anchored Volume by Price
- Raindrops
- The Scanner and the Strategy Tester

A big thank you to the good folks at TrendSpider!

Join thousands of trading students at New Trader University! Our eCourses are created for traders just starting out in the markets, and individuals looking to up their trading game.
Visit NewTraderUniversity.com to learn more about our eCourses today!

Don't forget that you can listen to many of our titles on Audible!

Read more of our bestselling titles:

The Working Dead
New Trader Rich Trader (Revised and Updated)
New Trader Rich Trader 2
So You Want to be a Trader
New Trader 101
Moving Averages 101: 2nd Edition
Options 101
5 Moving Averages That Beat Buy and Hold
Buy Signals and Sell Signals
Trading Habits
Investing Habits
Calm Trader

www.ingramcontent.com/pod-product-compliance
Lightning Source LLC
Chambersburg PA
CBHW060851220526
45466CB00003B/1331